lief

A Pocket Guide to Christian Belief

Dr Benno van den Toren

A Lion book
An imprint of
Lion Hudson plc
Wilkinson House,
Jordan Hill Road,
Oxford OX2 8DR, England

ISBN 978 0 7459 5214 7 (UK)
ISBN 978 0 8254 7863 5 (US)

Distributed by:
UK: Marston Book Services, PO Box 269, Abingdon, Oxon, OX14 4YN
USA: Trafalgar Square Publishing, 814 N. Franklin Street, Chicago, IL 60610
Christian Market: Kregel Publications, PO Box 2607, Grand Rapids, MI 49501

First edition 2009
10 9 8 7 6 5 4 3 2 1 0

Acknowledgments
Scripture taken from the Holy Bible, Today's New International® Version
TNIV©. Copyright 2001, 2005 by International Bible Society®. Used by
permission of International Bible Society®. All rights reserved worldwide.
'TNIV' and 'Today's New International Version' are trademarks registered in the
United States Patent and Trademark Office by International Bible Society®.

A catalogue record for this book is available from the British Library

Typeset in 10/12.5 Palatino
Printed in and bound in Malta

Contents

Preface

This pocket guide aims to provide an introduction to Christian belief. It describes the core convictions foundational to the Christian religion. There is of course much more to Christianity. Those other aspects may catch the eye of interested onlookers: Christian art and architecture, Christian worship and Christian institutions, Christian living and Christian social values. All of these merit introductions for their own sake. Yet none of these can be understood without reference to the unique centre of the Christian faith, without reference to what Christians believe about their relationship with God, about what Jesus Christ has done for them, about how this inspires them and gives them hope and a sense of direction. This is the basis of their self-identity and of how they live their lives.

This guide aims to introduce its readers to the unique Christian perspective on life, on the world and on God, realizing that people may have many different reasons for exploring it. Christianity has been a major cultural force in the world, and it is hard to understand all those Christian thinkers, artists and activists in the past and in the contemporary world when one lacks a basic grasp of their faith. It may also be that people want to appreciate what drives Christian movements or Christian family and friends in their immediate environment. These movements and people are of course often driven by some of the same basic human needs as other people and movements, and may not always be very different. Yet in many other ways Christians are different from the world around them. To outsiders, Christians often seem a strange bunch of people, sometimes all right, sometimes inspiring, sometimes irritating, but all too often plainly strange, particularly when non-Christians think about what Christians believe.

This guide hopes to offer some basic insight into why this Christian perspective on life is so important to them and why it makes sense to them. We all have the experience of meeting people or reading about people and thinking: why on earth do they believe this and live like this? It just seems so senseless, surreal or irrelevant. The fact is that these reactions show that we have not yet understood that person or position, for people ordinarily hold certain convictions because it makes sense to them. We can start criticizing people fairly only when we first understand why what they believe makes sense to them. I will consider that this book has been successful if people unfamiliar with Christianity have read it and understood why this movement has been so important to its followers, why it has had so much impact in history and why it is so important for people in many different cultural contexts today. This approach may also prove unexpectedly fertile in helping Christians to understand their own faith better, but they are not the first audience for which I have written it.

In this pocket guide, I will sketch what is sometimes called 'mere Christianity': not any specific form of Christianity that is at home only in the Western world or in the specific context of my own Christian tradition. I want to set out what has also been called 'the historic Christian faith': those central features of the Christian faith that have been shared across the ages and cultural boundaries. This cannot, however, be the largest common denominator of all those who call themselves Christian. Every religious community draws some lines, and so does the Christian community. Not all those who use the label 'Christian' can justifiably do so in the sense of belonging to the worldwide Christian community. People can go off track and make the label less meaningful. I therefore want to use the reality of Jesus Christ as we meet him in the Christian Scriptures as the standard by which to assess specific understandings of this faith. This means that I sometimes limit myself to what I consider the general Christian position and that in other instances I outline differences between various Christian traditions or different cultural expressions of Christianity. Though I have lived on different continents and in different cultural contexts, my sketch is unavoidably coloured in many ways by my own cultural contexts and by my own efforts to make sense of the meaning of the Christian faith and of the person of Jesus Christ. He has had an enormous impact on my life. I hope, however, that this limited perspective will open a window on a much wider reality, the reality of Jesus of Nazareth, whom Christians of all times and places believe to be the Lord and Saviour of the world.

This introduction will regularly refer to passages of the Bible, the Christian Scriptures. I use a recent English translation called *Today's New International Version*, but readers who want to look up some of the passages can easily use other translations. Translations vary in the style and vocabulary they use, and some are more precise or more accessible than others. Yet these variations in translation have relatively little impact on the message of the Bible itself, and different translations can therefore be used side by side. Reference to the Bible will have a form like 'John 17' or 'John 17:15–16'. 'John' is one of the sixty-six shorter books that make up the Bible, and can be found in its table of contents. The figure '17' is the chapter of the individual book, and '15–16' refers to the 'verses' that form subdivisions of the chapter, each verse normally containing just one sentence or part of a longer sentence. The second reference above would therefore mean 'The book of John, chapter 17, verses 15 to 16'.

Introduction: The Global Impact of Jesus of Nazareth

Global Christianity

As the title of this book is *A Pocket Guide to Christian Belief*, it seems appropriate to approach the subject by explaining the convictions of those who adhere to the Christian religion. Christians understand themselves as being part of Christian communities which are defined by a number of core beliefs that hold them together and make up their identity. Such a matter-of-fact understanding of 'Christian belief' is, however, not without its difficulties. What are the common beliefs that define people as 'Christian'? Through the centuries and across the globe, people who have considered themselves Christians and communities that have labelled themselves as Christian seem at first sight to have hardly anything in common and to hold a great variety of beliefs.

Christian belief across the centuries

The earliest Christians in the first century were mainly Jews, living in Jerusalem. With the larger Jewish community of the time, they worshipped in the Jerusalem Temple, circumcised their sons and kept to traditional Jewish purity laws concerning food and many other aspects of everyday life. They distinguished themselves from the larger Jewish community mainly because they saw in Jesus of Nazareth the promised Messiah, the anointed King and Liberator whom the Jews had been waiting for.

Within one generation, most new believers were from a non-Jewish background. When they came to believe in Jesus they were turning their backs on the Greco-Roman religious universe with its many gods: regional gods, personal gods and gods that represented the power of the Roman Empire. To these new Christians the Jewish notion of 'Messiah' made little sense. They related to Jesus primarily as their 'Lord', the one who had supreme authority over the universe and over their lives. Furthermore, they worshipped him as the 'Son of God', as the presence of the Creator of the universe himself, who had chosen to live among his own creatures.

The Christian faith soon moved to the north and west to the barbaric peoples of Central and Western Europe, beyond the borders of the political and cultural sphere of the Roman Empire. Many of the new Christians came from what we would nowadays call 'tribal' or 'primal' religions. They saw themselves as living in a universe filled with spiritual forces from which they looked for protection to Jesus as the great warrior who battled for them in the spiritual world. They saw him as a guide to an eternal home beyond the fleeting and uncertain nature of their earthly existence. They found in him the strength to fight against the pride and lust that pulled them away from what is truly worthwhile.

In the early centuries of the second millennium, these barbaric regions of Europe became the new heartlands of Christianity. And when modern Europe developed through the time of the Renaissance and the Reformation, Jesus Christ remained the guiding light of most of Europe's great thinkers. The European Age of Reason was in certain quarters highly critical of the traditional Christianity of the time, but for many modern thinkers Jesus himself remained the expression of all that was true and good. Jesus continued to be proclaimed, sometimes as the supreme example of reason and neighbourly love – the great ideals of modernity – but sometimes also in opposition to the forces of modernity. In an increasingly secular world, Jesus 'the lover of my soul' was proclaimed as the answer to the spiritual needs neglected by modernity, but also as the Lord and Liberator of the secular world itself.

Christian belief across the globe

Christianity never was an exclusively European religion. Before it established itself in Western and Northern Europe, it spread across North Africa and moved south along the Nile. It spread south to the Arabian peninsula and north toward Armenia. It moved east beyond the borders of the Roman Empire and soon established itself in India and then across Central Asia, reaching the borders of China over land. Even when the heartlands of Christianity lay in Europe, there were major Christian centres in Egypt, Turkey and the Middle East.

What is equally important is that the European variety of Christianity did not remain bounded by that continent. During the Middle Ages it was isolated because of the presence of Islamic empires toward the south and east, but with the beginning of the Modern Era, around the year 1500, it embarked on a new period of expansion. With the Spanish and Portuguese conquests it moved to South America and the Philippines. With the colonization of North America it took on new expressions on the continent which, from a European perspective, was the 'New World'. In conjunction with the explorations of Asia and Africa, large numbers of Christian missionaries went to those continents too.

The precise relationship of this missionary movement with Western colonial expansion is hugely contested. On the one hand, missionaries often profited from the colonialist presence and structures, and the colonial powers often saw Christian missionaries as allies in their efforts to pacify populations. Many Christians wholeheartedly believed that Western civilization was the fruit of Christian influence and that it was therefore no more than normal to share the blessings of this civilization together with the blessings of the gospel. On the other hand, many missionaries were highly critical of the dehumanizing colonial policies. The missionary movement was also a crucial force in the preservation of indigenous non-Western cultures, particularly through its efforts to translate the Bible into non-Western languages. These translation efforts showed respect for the receiving cultures and helped preserve these languages and the cultures they bore. The mission schools were a principal breeding ground for a new generation of non-Western leaders who took the lead in the decolonization movement in the twentieth century.

As it turned out, the Western missionary movement led to the renewal of the Christian faith as a non-Western religion. Western missionaries had only limited influence on the Christianity they planted. The crucial actors were the first and second generations of Christians in those new worlds who understood the Christian faith in their own ways. From the missionary message, they selected those elements which they found most helpful in their own context. They started reading the freshly translated Christian Scriptures by themselves and relating the Jesus they encountered there to their own questions and to their own worlds. Thus the Christian belief of the Latino Catholics has a very different flavour from the Southern European Catholicism from which it originated. British Anglicans would hardly recognize the exuberant faith their missionaries sowed in Africa. Brazilian Pentecostal Christians have a social impact which may have exceeded not only the expectations but also the interest of North American Pentecostals. Christian minorities in the multi-religious contexts of South-East Asia need to express themselves in ways that differ radically from expressions of Christianity found in the predominantly Christian continents.

As a consequence, one can now say that in certain respects Christianity is the first religion which can claim to be truly a world religion. Other world religions such as Hinduism and Buddhism have remained concentrated in certain regions of the world, and if they have moved out of those regions it is mainly due to the migration of Chinese and Indian populations across the globe. The spread of Christianity has also greatly profited from the mass migration of Christian populations, but in the process it has in an unprecedented way crossed ethnic and cultural divides. Its heartlands and predominant expressions have moved across the globe: from Jerusalem where it originated, via Byzantium and Rome, to Northern Europe and North America. Today, parallel to the diminishing Christian influence in the northern hemisphere, we see an unprecedented growth in the South, with new centres in cities such as São Paulo, Lagos and Seoul. In this respect Christianity also differs from Islam, which has also seen fast growth, sometimes faster than Christianity. But in its normative forms Islam has remained an Arab religion with its geographical centre in the old cities of Mecca and Medina. This is partly because, according to the traditional view, to get deeper into Islam you need to learn the Arab language and assimilate the Arab culture, as the Qur'an cannot be translated from the divine Arabic in which it was written. This contrasts with the continuing translation of the Christian Scriptures into different languages and their consequent expression in the new cultural worlds.

The impact of Jesus of Nazareth

Common threads

Christianity has therefore entered an exciting new phase in its history. It shows an amazing vigour and adaptability to new contexts. Its Western expressions have become less normative and are enriched by a dazzling variety of lively new Christian communities. On the one hand Christianity is thereby freed from its close association with Northern Atlantic culture. This association had provided some of its strength, but has also become an increasing liability because of the secularization of the West, because of Western imperialism and because of the increasing influence of other major civilizations. However, this raises with new urgency the question brought up in the beginning of this introductory chapter: can one in any meaningful sense speak of 'Christian belief', when we encounter this belief in such numerous and radically different forms across the globe and throughout the religion's historical development?

In recent times few thinkers have been so impressed by the amazing variety of Christianity across the ages and the globe as Professor Andrew Walls, a specialist in the study of Christianity in the non-Western world. Yet, in his publications, he has noted that these varied expressions have a few very important things in common. In the first place, all these communities share the same Holy Scriptures. There may be slight variations as to the number of books they consider as authoritative, and there may be discussions over translations and interpretations. But by and large the Scriptures are shared, and have been the basis of meaningful dialogue between Christians from very different backgrounds. Secondly, Christians across the centuries have considered themselves members of a community which spans the ages and the continents. They basically understand themselves as part of the one people of God and, as such, in the line of the Old Testament people of Israel and the earliest Christians in Jerusalem. Thirdly, they believe that they worship one God, the Creator of the universe, who made himself known to his people, to Israel and to the church.

Finally and most significantly, all Christians consider Jesus of Nazareth to be of ultimate importance. They may give him different titles in their day-to-day worship, but by these titles they are all giving him the central role in their relationship with God. When they call him Lord they are giving him the highest authority over their lives. They approach him as their Saviour and the Saviour of the world, whichever way this salvation may be understood. The wide variety of expressions of the Christian faith in history and today are all a result of the impact of this one person, Jesus of Nazareth. Faith in him has apparently so much to offer that all those communities can relate to him in many different ways and yet the meaning of this single life has not been exhausted. He is welcomed as the promised Messiah, worshipped as Son of God, embraced as the Lover of the soul. To him people across the ages look as their Saviour, Protector and Healer. He is proclaimed as Master and Lord, and in him people continue to find deep meaning and fulfilment.

'Christian belief' as a normative idea

Within the variety of expressions of the Christian faith, we can therefore perceive a number of common threads which justify our talk of 'Christian belief' in the singular. For Christians, moreover, 'Christian belief' is more than just a description of their actual beliefs, which may indeed differ from one Christian community to another. The four commonalities pointed out by Walls all point to the fact that Christians see themselves as relating to a reality that surpasses their particular beliefs and understanding: they believe that there is a God who exists independently of their belief and who was there before there even was a Christian community. They believe in their Scriptures as a normative revelation of who this God is and of his plan for the world. They believe that their faith is founded on Jesus Christ and that who this Jesus truly was is more important for them than what they have made of him. They believe that they are not the first to know God, but that there is a community across the ages to which they relate and from which they can learn.

Christians have indeed had a tendency to take their own traditions and understandings for granted. Yet they have also remembered that their own understandings and traditions are not the final authority, and in virtually all Christian communities there is an ongoing critical reflection on whether they have truly understood God for who he is or whether they have made their own projection of God according to their needs and expectations. What the Christian communities across the ages have in common provides them with a standard against which to assess their own understandings of their faith. They recognize Christ as their Lord, to whom they desire to submit both their lives and convictions. They have the Scriptures as the final authority over their lives and beliefs. They are part of, and can learn from, a Christian community across the ages and across the globe. This last element provides a critical resource from which the Christian community can profit as never before. Never before has the Christian community known so many different cultural expressions. Never before has there been so much opportunity for communication between Christian communities from different parts of the world.

A stranger, who makes himself at home in every world

'Christian belief' is therefore not just a label for what actual Christians do believe. For Christians themselves it encapsulates what they should believe, and points to the reality which they aspire to understand and to which they seek to adapt their actual beliefs. This explains why Christianity as we find it in history has always had a dual relationship with the surrounding culture and communities. This has often been explained in the words of Jesus himself, who said of his disciples that they were in the world, yet not of the world (John 17:11, 16). Christian communities are part of the world in which they live. They believe that this is the world their God created, that this is the world over which Christ is Lord and which he came to save. Christians are part of their culture and to a certain degree they share its aspirations. They want to relate Jesus Christ to the convictions and the questions of that culture to which they belong. Christ can be Lord only if his authority is recognized over all the areas of the culture in which they live. He can be Saviour only if his salvation impacts the lives they used to live in that world and the life they still have in common with those around them. We therefore see a continuous pattern of Jesus Christ entering into different cultures and of the Christian faith being adapted to different cultural contexts. This explains the wide variety of expressions of the Christian faith through the ages and in the worldwide Christian community.

Yet, even though the followers of Christ are 'in this world', they are not 'of this world'. They do not entirely belong to the world and remain strangers to this world. They remain strangers because, and to the extent that, the message of Jesus Christ is strange within every cultural context. Christians believe that Jesus Christ gives a radically new perspective on life and a radically different answer to the challenges of life than the other answers on offer. Christ is therefore critical to the way people understand their world and live their lives. Accepting Christ always entails some kind of conversion, some radical change in the way people understand and direct their lives. This is why Christians, despite their variety, still consider themselves part of one new people. This is why we can perceive not just Christianity appearing in ever new forms, but also perceive a universalizing principle in Christian history, by which Christians are drawn out of their particular communities to a common understanding of their lives, which they discover through their encounter with Christ and their entry in the worldwide church.

Christ can therefore make himself at home in every culture, yet he always remains a stranger, making people regard themselves and their cultures in a new way. This is why Jesus Christ always remains a critical measure by which every cultural expression of the Christian faith must be assessed. Christians believe that what makes them Christian is not some inherited label, or the mere fact of their continuity with the historical Christian community. What makes them Christian is their relationship with Jesus Christ as their Lord and Saviour. The reality of Christ, limited as their perception and understanding of it may be, therefore always remains the standard by which to critique their own understanding of their faith.

Thinking about Christian belief

The 'strange new world' of the Christian faith

It is not easy to provide a good description of Christian belief. It has so many aspects that every perspective is in certain respects one-sided. That is why Christians across the world look to Christians of other times and places so that their own understanding may be enlarged and deepened. An equally serious obstacle to providing an adequate description of the Christian faith is that it is all too easy to understand and explain it in terms of what we already know, in line with the kind of knowledge with which we are acquainted. The Christian faith has been understood as an example of a worldview, as a form of the psychological mechanisms people use to cope with the hardships and uncertainties of life, as a social project, as an expression of the mystical depths of life, as a religion. We start from a reality which we think we understand – say, religions or psychological coping mechanisms – and we interpret Christianity as an instance of it.

The problem is that the Christian faith is none of these. Of course Christianity has much in common with other religions and worldviews, it helps us to cope psychologically, and it encompasses a social project. But it is much more than can be described in terms of psychology or sociology. It breaks open every preconceived idea of what a religion or a worldview are like. It challenges predetermined notions of the mystical nature of life. Christians claim that Christianity does indeed relate to many common experiences, maybe to all of them. It provides an answer to the religious quest of humanity; it addresses psychological and social needs. That is why this book and so many books on Christianity are not all that strange but relate to many common experiences. Yet everyone who studies the Christian faith must be ready for surprises, for new light unexpectedly falling on familiar experiences.

To study the Christian faith, then, is to enter a 'new world' or even a 'strange new world'. This expression, coined by the Swiss thinker Karl Barth, is a particularly apt description of what happens when we study Christian belief. To explore it in all its strangeness and unfamiliarity will mean resisting the urge to understand it in terms of known categories. And we will need to resist the temptation to think that we already understand the basics of this faith because of what we have seen of it. This may be true, but we should also be open to the fact that even the basics may be much richer or stranger than we thought they would be. We need to enter this world with the curiosity of an explorer who enters unfamiliar territory. We need to be ready to make sense of the elements of the Christian faith not in terms of what we already know, but in terms of this world itself. Jesus Christ, for example, may not at first make sense in terms of the expectations we bring to religious leaders, but he does make sense in the realm to which he belongs. He makes sense in relation to the Christian understanding of God and of his project with the universe.

This introduction to Christian belief is an invitation to enter this new world. It is a place that is foreign to many of the other contexts from which we may come. Yet to enter it will enable us to look back at the ordinary world in which we live and understand how Christians make sense of the many experiences that are common to all.

Why truth matters for Christians

This book does not claim to give a new perspective on the Christian faith. It simply aims to summarize and share some of the thinking about the faith which has been developing for almost two thousand years. In doing that, we can draw on an extraordinarily rich tradition of reflection on the Christian faith. Christian thinkers have always had a particular interest in the truth of their fundamental beliefs. The Christian faith is a way of life, but not just a way of life. As a way of life it is based on a number of fundamental convictions about the way the world is. Christian thinkers have therefore spent much time reflecting on those fundamental convictions, what they mean and whether they are justified. They felt that their life depended on it.

It may seem obvious that Christian thinkers are interested in the truth of their fundamental beliefs. However, when we compare Christianity with other religions, we discover that this interest is specific to Christianity and is itself related to a number of core Christian convictions about who God is and how he relates to us.

When we compare the Christian faith with Hinduism and Buddhism as the main Eastern religions, we see that the latter are much less interested in questions of religious truth. More precisely, many Hindu and Buddhist thinkers would consider it impossible to say anything definitive about the divine reality. The divine is beyond what humans can comprehend and what can be expressed in human words. It would be futile to try to do so. It lies beyond human polarities of light and darkness, truth and error, male and female, good and evil. Religious experience also seems by nature diffuse and hard to articulate. Many contemporary Westerners who are not necessarily Hindus or Buddhists would resonate with this understanding of religious reality and religious experience: if God exists at all, people can never claim any definite knowledge of him/her/it.

Christians, however, do not consider it pretentious to believe otherwise. They do not claim to be more spiritual or more capable of understanding the divine. The difference between Christianity and Eastern thought is rather based on a different understanding of God. For Christians, their understanding of God is not based on some high-quality religious experience. It originates in the desire of God himself to make himself known to humankind. God himself has chosen to show who he is by sending Jesus and by giving humankind the Christian Scriptures. In the process, he has shown himself to be not an ineffable reality or a diffuse entity beyond all logic and contradictions, but to be a definable person. Christians realize that they can never grasp God entirely, but hold that God himself has given them reasons to believe that certain expressions describe his character better than others, and that certain things should never be ascribed to God. 'God is light; in him there is no darkness at all' (1 John 1:5); God is love in his very nature, and even when Christians ascribe hatred to God, this should be understood as the obverse of his love, as the rejection of all that hinders the expression of his love in the world. Truth about God matters, because God has revealed the truth about himself to the world.

Yet another aspect of the Christian preoccupation with truth becomes apparent when we compare it with Islam. Like Christianity and unlike the Eastern religions, Islam places great stress on revelation: Allah has sent his prophets in order to call humankind back from the many gods which they worshipped to the one Creator of the universe; these prophets gave his commandments to humankind, so that it might live accordingly. Yet Muslim and Christian theologians agree that there is an important difference between their respective understandings of revelation. According to the Qur'an, God has revealed his commandments – his will – in order to show humankind how to live according to this will. He has not, however, revealed *himself*; it should be enough for us to know his *will*. How could we want more of the King of the universe? Accordingly, religious specialists in Islam are primarily interpreters of the *Sharia*, the divine law, and explore the will of God for every detail of life.

According to Christians, God revealed not just his will, but also himself. He wants people to know him personally. In Islam, the main model for the relationship between God and humanity is the relationship between a master and his slaves. A slave needs only to know the will of his master. The God of the Bible calls human beings his children, his friends and even his bride. He desires an intimate relationship with them, and that is why he has revealed himself and his love for humankind. Religious specialists in the Christian tradition are therefore not specialists in the will of God. They reflect on who God himself is and what his plan for the world is. They are rightly called 'theologians' (from the Greek for 'God' and 'reason'), people who think about God: they use all their intellectual powers to seek to understand what God has made known of himself. They respond gratefully and humbly to this incredible initiative of God to make himself known.

There is a second difference between Christianity and Islam that helps us understand why Christians are so concerned about questions of truth. Like Muslim thinkers, Christians explore the law of God, how God wants us to live (see chapter 7). Yet the Christian exploration of what the Christian life should look like is based on what God has done for humanity. Christians have a profound conviction that however human beings organize their lives, they can never free themselves from their predicament. For their salvation they depend entirely on God. Salvation is not a consequence of how they organize their lives. Salvation is first and foremost based on what God has done for them. Christian theological thinking therefore does not limit itself to reflection on who God is, but takes a specific interest in what God has done in order to save humanity from sin and death, from the mess in which humankind finds itself. Christian thinkers give particular attention to what God has done for humanity, because their salvation, their future, the meaning of their life, depend on it.

Orthodoxy in context

This is also why Christian theologians have traditionally been much occupied with questions of so-called 'orthodoxy' and 'heresy'. 'Orthodoxy' is shorthand for the true faith of the

Christian community, while 'heresy' stands for those deviant opinions that are believed to undermine the essentials of the Christian faith. Because of this, the church has traditionally excluded heretics from their community. It was thought that they were a danger to what was most precious to their community.

This idea that people can exclude others from a community because of their beliefs is of course hugely unpopular in today's world, which champions tolerance for all. We can, however, better understand this interest in maintaining orthodoxy when we realize that for Christians their salvation and their identity as a community depend on certain beliefs that they consider essential. It depends, for example, on the convictions that God has truly made himself known in Jesus Christ and that he has conquered the powers of death and evil. If these beliefs were not true, there could be no salvation in a Christian sense, and when members of the community deny those essential beliefs, they undermine its very identity. It may well be that Christians have often called others 'heretics' in order to fight their private battles or because they lacked the capacity to recognize that God's truth is larger than they thought. However, the Christian idea of salvation demands that some limits be set to what can justly be called Christian. And as in any healthy community, the Christian community will also want to define what beliefs its members may validly hold without undermining what is essential to its life and identity.

So far, our exploration of the many different forms that Christian belief has taken in the course of history and across the world suggests that the Christian search for truth cannot be directed at finding a monolithic and timeless expression of what the Christian faith is about. Christian theology, Christian reflection on its faith, always moves between two poles. On the one hand it orients itself to the reality of God – to the self-revelation of God in Jesus Christ, who always remains the critical measure against which Christians must evaluate what they have made of him. On the other hand, Christian theology orients itself to its particular cultural context. It asks what the meaning of the message of Jesus Christ is for the particular world in which this Christian community finds itself. What might the impact of Jesus of Nazareth be for this community? How can he be Lord and Saviour in this particular world? How can he bring this community back to the one Creator of all humankind?

1. How Do We Know God?

God makes himself known

It is incredibly daring to claim to know anything about God. It is daring in light of who God is: if there is a God, there is every reason to expect him to be far beyond our limited human comprehension. It is equally daring in the light of the religious diversity we perceive around us. The religions make different and often contradictory claims about the divine. Some believe that there is one God, others that there are many. Some believe that there is a personal God who relates to us in a personal manner, others that the divine is an impersonal 'ground of being' and that we can only relate to it in so far as we relinquish our individual personality. At first sight it may seem counterintuitive that human beings would ever be able to evaluate such contrasting claims. Where can we find a compass to orientate us in the fleeting world of religious experiences?

Christians answer this question with the help of the notion of revelation. 'Revelation' is a technical term referring to the belief that God makes himself known. If Christians claim to have access to any sort of knowledge of God, it is because they believe that God himself has taken the initiative to make himself known to humanity. Christians do not claim to have better religious antennae than adherents of other religions, or to be more morally pure so that they deserve some privileged knowledge of God. It is only because, out of his own will and love for humanity, God has decided to make himself known that they find courage to say anything about him.

The fact that knowledge of God rests on his initiative has an important consequence. It means that human beings have no way of knowing beforehand what this revelation should look like. They cannot come up with some preconceived idea about how God should reveal himself and then subsequently look for it where they think such revelation might materialize. If revelation is God's initiative, it is he who decides whether, how and where he reveals himself. Human beings have very little to go on when they want to know what to look for. It is only when they are confronted with the reality of God's self-revelation that they can start thinking seriously about what this revelation is like and how God reveals himself. Christians claim that such self-revelation of God can be encountered in the Bible and in Jesus of Nazareth.

In order to understand revelation, we therefore need to start with some particular instance of where revelation is claimed to be found. Does this imply, however, that Christians are caught in circular reasoning because they need to start with an initial belief that God does indeed reveal himself in the Bible and in Jesus? Christians do not think that this necessarily leads them into a position in which they would have to accept every purported claim to revelation. A comparison may make this clear. Imagine that someone claims to have discovered a new archaeological site that contains objects that would bring us into contact with a hitherto unknown ancient civilization. Obviously, there is no way of finding out whether these claims are true other than by doing the necessary digging and starting with the available archaeological evidence. But that does not mean that we need to accept everything at face value. We may still consider whether these artefacts truly belong to an ancient civilization or whether they are counterfeits placed there more recently simply to make us believe in such an ancient culture. And even when we are confronted with artefacts from a hitherto unknown civilization, we would need to consider them carefully, asking whether they tell us significant things about this civilization, or simply demonstrate that there must have been a civilization, though it remains shrouded in mystery. In the process we would of course be greatly helped if we found written sources, and if, after deciphering the new script and language, we found we had stumbled across some of the foundational narratives of this society.

In what follows, we will therefore look at those places where, according to Christians, God can be known.

Revelation in history

A history of covenants

As we will see later, Christians believe that it is possible to gain a glimpse of God's existence, power and wisdom by looking at nature. This is often referred to as God's 'general revelation'. God has chosen to make himself known through his creation. We will also see, however, that Christians believe that nature can reveal only a limited knowledge of God and in some ways actually hinders our understanding of him. When asked how they know God, Christians will therefore first of all point to God's self-revelation in history. This is normally called 'special revelation'.

This history begins with Abraham. Abraham and his family lived somewhere in Mesopotamia (currently Iraq) at the beginning of the second millennium before Christ (some time after 2000 BC). His story is told in Genesis, the first book of the Christian Bible. Abraham and his family were called to leave their community and home country in order to search for a new land that God promised to give them. It later becomes clear that Canaan was this promised land, a small country east of the Mediterranean, where we currently find Israel and Palestine. It would never have become widely known had it not been for the special place it was given in the history of God's relationship with humankind.

This special relationship between God and Abraham is called a 'covenant', in which God promised to make Abraham a great nation. Abraham, in turn, was invited to enter into a privileged relationship with the one God and to renounce all other gods. His family and the people that grew out of it were singled out from among all the peoples around them, and their life was to reflect this special relationship. An important characteristic of this covenant relationship is that Abraham and his family were not just chosen for their own sakes. God said to him in Genesis 12:2–3:

> *I will make you into a great nation,*
> *   and I will bless you;*
> *I will make your name great,*
> *   and you will be a blessing.*
> *I will bless those who bless you,*
> *   and whoever curses you I will curse;*
> *and all peoples on earth*
> *   will be blessed through you.*

God entered into this special relationship so that throughout the course of history all the nations of the earth could be blessed through Abraham and his descendants.

The scandal of particularity

The choice or election of one group for the benefit of the whole world is equally clear in God's history with the people of Israel, which descended from Abraham and with whom God also entered into a covenant relationship. Only two generations after Abraham arrived in Canaan, his descendants became economic refugees in nearby Egypt, then one of the most powerful nations on earth. There they were increasingly suppressed by the dominant Egyptian population, which ended up exploiting them as slaves. Because of his special covenant relationship with Abraham, God then called Moses to lead this people out of slavery in Egypt, involving a perilous journey across the desert, back to Canaan, the land of promise. This liberation is known as the 'exodus' and is the foundational event for Israel as a nation, still celebrated yearly in the Jewish feast of Passover.

In the desert between Egypt and Canaan, at a mountain called Sinai, God entered into a covenant relationship with this people, similar to the covenant with Abraham. He chose the people of Israel to have this special relationship with him, to be his people, but in turn Israel was placed under a number of covenant obligations towards God. They were given a collection of laws, both moral and religious, that marked them out from the nations among which they lived. These laws had a number of functions. They were aimed at helping them to live according to God's plan for them. God gave these laws so that they might truly live as a liberated people and flourish as he intended. As such, Israel was also meant to be an example for the peoples around them. When God chose Israel he was not forgetting the other nations. In its special relationship with God, Israel was meant to live out what it means to live a truly human life, the life for which God had created humanity as a whole. These laws, furthermore, functioned to guard them as a distinct people with a clear identity among the peoples around them, a people through which God could work for the well-being of the entire world.

From the very beginning of the Bible and from the moment he called Abraham, God is presented as the God of the whole universe. God had chosen to enter into a specific relationship with humanity and to execute his rescue plan for humanity beginning with one family and one people. This is sometimes referred to as 'the scandal of particularity'. In a number of religions, particularly in Eastern religions, it is believed that the divine is equally present in all. That of course resonates well with modern Western expectations that everyone should be treated equally. In that light Judaism and Christianity are often frowned upon because they claim that God entered into this special, privileged relationship with the people of Israel and now with the church. We cannot stress enough that Israel and the church have this special position only to benefit the whole world. They are like an experimental garden in which everyone should be able to see God's aims for humanity as a whole. This means that the calling of Israel and the church is not just a privilege, but also an enormous responsibility. It is sad that Israel and the church have often been so little different from the rest of the world. This experimental garden has often been overgrown with weeds and has become as much of a jungle as the surrounding land. Israel and the church have often failed in their vocation.

The God of history

The belief that God has made himself known in a special way to a specific community is related to another defining characteristic of the Christian understanding of God: he is the God and Liberator of history. This God does not aim for an exclusively spiritual relationship with humanity. He is not content with saving souls and guiding them out of this world to a spiritual realm of eternal bliss. This God is deeply concerned about how people live their lives in the mess and hardship of this world. This became clear when he liberated Israel out of its slavery in Egypt – showing himself to be moved by the suffering and freedom of his people.

The liberation of Israel from Egypt is a defining feature of a history which still continues. Christians believe that God is still at work in history for the liberation of humankind. God's project of liberation is too great to be limited to Israel and to the problem of its socioeconomic and cultural oppression in Egypt. God is at work in history, and this project will be finished only when, at the end of history, the whole earth – even the whole universe – will be renewed, and when all the peoples of the earth will live in freedom and harmony.

In this respect, the Christian faith is radically different from both religions and secular self-help movements which promote freedom through spiritual insights and spiritual encounters. There is no doubt that spiritual insights are crucial in the pilgrimage to freedom and to full humanity. Such insights, however, are not enough for people who live in oppression and slavery; they are not enough for the mother who sees her child die of hunger or a lack of proper medication. Christians believe in a God who is concerned about those aspects of life and who is doing something about it. This history which started with Abraham and Israel will be finished only when all the peoples of the earth are reached with this message and have encountered the liberating power of God.

Jesus as God's ultimate self-revelation

Christians believe that God's history of revealing himself to humanity reached its culmination in Jesus Christ, a Jewish man living in Palestine, through whom God's history with Israel impacted the whole world. It is this conviction that God revealed himself decisively and most clearly in Jesus that is the defining feature of the Christian religion. This also marks it out from Judaism, which in other aspects is the closest to it. Both religions believe that God was acting and revealing himself in his history with Israel, and many Jews would subscribe to most of what was said about God's revelation in the earlier sections of this chapter. Judaism and Christianity differ, however, in that Christians believe that the history of God with Israel culminated in Jesus of Nazareth. In Jesus God revealed himself in a radically new way which brought to its fulfilment the history leading up to it.

In Jesus God revealed himself in a new way as the Liberator and Saviour of humanity. For Christians the decisive event in the life of Jesus was not what he accomplished during his life, but his death. At the end of a short life in which he preached about the reign of God, he was executed on a cross under the authority of the Roman Empire. Christians believe, however, that his death was not the end, but that after three days God raised him again from the dead. He did not just come back to life, but entered into a new mode of life, a glorified eternal and imperishable life, which he wants to share with others. Here liberation means much more than deliverance from sociopolitical oppression as it happened in the exodus from Egypt. In the exodus itself and in the consequent history of Israel, it had already become clear that this liberation was also about being able to serve God in a new way and that it was ultimately meant to encompass all aspects of life.

In the cross and the resurrection of Jesus, liberation therefore takes on a whole new dimension. Christians believe that in these events God was acting to liberate humanity from the two greatest enemies of human life: sin and death. Sin, which alienates human beings from God and from fellow human beings, was dealt with on the cross of Jesus. Death, which is the enemy which finally brings every human project and life to nothing, was conquered in the resurrection of Jesus. These phrases are obviously loaded with meaning and not easy to understand. We will unpack them in a later chapter. For now it is important to note how in Christ God revealed himself again as the Liberator. This liberation is so all-encompassing in the way it deals with sin and death that Christians often use a different term with a wider and more specifically Christian meaning: in the cross and resurrection of Jesus, God revealed himself as our *Saviour*.

In Jesus Christ, God did not just demonstrate what he was doing for the salvation of humankind. Christians believe that God also revealed *himself*. It is here that the word 'self-revelation', which we have been using, has its most profound meaning. We have already noted in the introduction that the Christian God does not just reveal his will for humankind, but that he reveals himself, because he wants humanity to know and love him in return. Christians see this self-revelation of God most clearly in Jesus. They consider him to be not just as a wise man or a prophet, but God himself, who came to live in the world and share his life with human beings. This is a mind-blowing idea, particularly for Jews, who believe that God and humanity, the Creator and his creation, are radically distinct. It is not as if one morning a couple of followers of Jesus thought it would be a great idea to start thinking about Jesus as God. It was incredibly hard for them to start regarding Jesus in that way. But the Jesus they had lived with when he walked among them, and the living Lord who was still present among them after his death and resurrection, did not fit any of the categories they had available for him. The reality of this man forced them to start thinking of him as God. We will come back to this amazing and often puzzling feature of the Christian faith in chapter 5.

Jesus is God's presence among humanity, God becoming human so that he could relate to human beings and they could relate to him in an entirely new way. He is not an *avatar* in the Hindu sense of a god appearing in human form. Christians believe that God can indeed appear in human form as he did once when he appeared to Abraham (Genesis 18). What happened in Jesus Christ was different. He was not just an outward form in which God appeared. Rather, God had become a human being, taken on human existence as his own, become 'God incarnate'. This is why this happened once and for all, as an unrepeatable event. A god can *appear* in many *avatars*, but truly *becoming* a human being can happen only once. We live only once, and cannot relive our lives, as much as we would sometimes want to do so. That God became a human being once and for all in Jesus of Nazareth is a consequence of his truly becoming a human being like us and not just appearing in a human form which he could shake off when he wanted. This throws even more light on the 'scandal of particularity' to which we referred before: the fact that God does not reveal himself equally to all and in all times, but that he has revealed himself most clearly at one specific place and time in history. This is because he wanted to reveal himself in this marvellous way by truly becoming a human being, so that humankind could in a sense meet him face to face.

This central Christian belief that God revealed himself supremely in sharing human existence also has major implications for how Christians see God. Because Jesus Christ lived a human life, they believe that God is not distant, but deeply involved with humanity and the world. Because Jesus Christ died a human death, Christians believe that God is not foreign to human suffering, but that he experienced it and shared it on the cross. A different group of questions is related to the fact that while God was present in Christ, he still remained the God who upheld the universe. While God was present in Jesus Christ, he was not limited to Jesus Christ. This led finally to the recognition of some form of multiplicity in God, more precisely of the recognition of three persons in God: the Father who created the world, the Son who lived among us in Jesus Christ, and the Holy Spirit who still fills and inspires the followers of Jesus. This resulted in the belief in the 'tri-unity' of God. Questions related to the tri-unity of God, God's relation to suffering and God's involvement in the world will be explored later on in this book.

Revelation through nature

God's revelation through nature and in the depth of the human soul

We began our exploration of the Christian understanding of God's self-revelation with God's special revelation in the history of Israel and in Jesus Christ. We have already indicated that Christians do not limit God's revelation to this special relationship with Israel and the church. Christians do not suppose that they are the only ones to know anything about God. The Bible itself makes clear that God has made himself known to all people. Christians believe that the God of the Bible is the Creator of the universe and that he shows himself in certain ways in what he has made. Just as a painting shows something of the painter, the beauty, the majesty and the complexity of the world show something of the power and wisdom of its Maker. People do not need complex philosophical arguments to come to that conclusion. Many people are overcome by a deep sense of awe when they ponder the beauty of nature and are convinced that there must be some sort of God who has made all this.

In a similar way, many people experience the care of God in the way they are provided with the basic needs of life and even more. Many people know moments when they are overcome with profound thankfulness, even if they would find it hard to know to whom or to what their gratitude should be directed. This sense of thankfulness may be provoked by a sudden realization of how abnormal it is that they are able to provide themselves with the daily needs of food and shelter. It may gain a new depth when people have an unexpected experience of love and companionship or receive new life in the form of a baby added to their family and community.

Christians also believe that God has made human beings with a deep need and longing for him. God wants them to know and love him and has therefore created them with an inner pull to search for him. People may not necessarily experience this as a need for God, but simply as a profound lack of satisfaction with the world and with life as it is that keeps pushing them forward and stops them from quietly settling with their existing lives. In the fourth chapter we will take some more time to explore the Christian understanding of this general human restlessness. In different ways God's creation and providence, and this longing, have provided people with a sense of God apart from God's special revelation in the history that began with Abraham.

The limits to what people can know through general revelation

Although most Christian thinkers would agree that human beings can know God to a certain degree through his general revelation, there is significant discussion with regard to what can be known about God in this way and about how reliable this knowledge is. Roman Catholic theologians tend to be more positive, and some have even built entire systems of what can be known about God from nature. Protestant theologians tend to be more hesitant and would place a greater stress on the way this revelation of God in nature is so often distorted and wrongly perceived, even blatantly denied. It is possible to say that there is no God at all. This suggests that even if God can be known through his creation, this revelation of himself is not so evident that it cannot be misunderstood.

Looking at the world around them with its many religions, Christians realize that they need a nuanced understanding of how God makes himself known through nature. On the one hand, Christians see the presence and vitality of religions in the world as a confirmation of the religious quest of humankind. Even atheistic countries with state-controlled education systems have not been able to erase this quest and this sense that there is a God. On the other hand, the contradictory religious claims about what God or the divine is like and wants from humankind, and the terrible things that have been done in the name of religion, make it unlikely that humankind has a reliable antenna to tune into the divine. The religions continue to be a major reason in themselves for the appeal of atheistic rejections of all belief in God.

Christian thinkers have given different reasons for the profoundly ambiguous nature of what can be known about God from nature. In the first place, this world is made by God, but it is not itself divine. We cannot see the Creator himself, but only his work. It is therefore possible to believe that this world exists by itself and because of itself. Thus the theory of evolution has been taken to mean that the evolving universe as we know it is the ultimate reality and that one needs no outside intelligence or power to explain its existence. We will return to the theory of evolution and the evolutionist understanding of the universe in chapter 3, and we will see how in some of its later developments Christians perceive indications that it can be reconciled with the Christian understanding of the universe as created; even more, that the belief in a Creator God may provide the best wider framework in which to make sense of the particular evolutionary universe in which we find ourselves.

In the second place, natural revelation is a wordless revelation. What people can know of God through religious experience and through their reflection on the created world is fairly vague and open-ended. It leaves therefore room for many different and contradicting interpretations. Many people have religious experiences, but how they interpret them is profoundly influenced by their cultural and religious background. An Arab Muslim will interpret religious experiences differently from a Javanese mystic, differently from someone nurtured in an African Traditional Religion, and differently again from an atheist. Their experiences themselves even differ because of the wider contexts in which they occur.

In the third place, this world in which humanity finds itself is not the world as God meant it to be. Human beings do not live in the loving relationship with their Creator that they are invited to live in. They have not been obedient to God's project for the world, but have rather rejected it. This has had disastrous consequences. It has brought evil in the world, and it means that we do not only experience the goodness that might lead us to a grateful recognition of the care of the Creator. Experiences of war, hatred, hunger and lack of basic human needs sometimes give the impression of a world which is abandoned rather than cared for. The reality of suffering makes it difficult to believe in a benevolent Creator God.

Because of sin, because humankind does not live with God as it was meant to do, people also have a tendency to neglect or even to suppress their deep need for God. They cannot face the void in their existence. Christian thinkers see the religions around them not only as a positive sign that human beings need God and have a sense of God, but also as distortions of what religion should be. Religions are often abused to further human projects and interests. Instead of living a religious life as an expression of a desire to know God, people often use religion as a way to promote self-interest and even to control and suppress the weak in society. Christian thinkers have been honest enough to recognize that Christianity itself has equally been abused in such ways.

Finally, according to Christians, God's revelation through nature can only tell us that there is a God and reveal something of his wisdom and power. It does not tell us anything of his plan for the universe. Christians believe that God has created humankind so that they may enter into a special relationship with him. Creation itself may drive human beings to seek fulfilment for their lives beyond anything that the created universe can provide. Nature cannot tell us, however, whether this fulfilment can actually be found in God. If God wants to enter into such a relationship of love with humankind, this is a special grace on his part. He is God and human beings have no claim on him. If he offers himself to them, so that they may know him, it can only be because he has freely chosen to do so. They can therefore know that God offers himself to be their Father and Friend only if he wants to do so and if he actually initiates such a relationship with them. For that relationship, they therefore depend on a special act, a special revelation from him. Nature can never tell them that God loves humankind so much.

The created world also does not tell of God's activity to redeem the world. We have already touched on the reality of sin; the fact that humans do not live according to God's project for them. We will see later how, according to Christians, sin has deeply marred human existence; how humankind has become alienated from God and from their true being. In fact, humankind has become enslaved to forces that keep them from loving God, from living in harmony with the world and with the people around them, and from finding their true selves (chapter 4). What people can know of God through his general revelation does not show how God has also taken the initiative to redeem humankind, to save it from the dire situation in which it finds itself. Much, maybe most, of the Christian message is precisely about this work of God to save humanity. That is why it understands itself as a 'gospel', a word meaning 'good news'. According to Christians this plan of salvation, how God has come to redeem humanity, is the best news humans can ever hear.

We have seen in this section how Christians believe that God has made himself known everywhere through the world he created, through his care for creation and through the 'seed of religion' he has sown in every human soul. What can be known about God through this general revelation is, however, severely limited, because of the mixed messages of a world in which they not only see the glory of God, but also imperfection and deep human suffering. What God shows of himself in this general way can also easily be manipulated, leading to humankind coming up with all sorts of images of God and the divine, even going so far as to declare itself the centre of the universe. Just as importantly, this general revelation of God does not tell humankind about his plan to redeem humanity and the universe, and does not permit them to enter into a personal relationship with him. Christians believe that they know these aspects of God only because he has made himself known in a special way in the history of Israel and the church.

The Holy Scriptures

In the light of the Christian understanding of God's self-revelation, it becomes clear why the Bible has such a central place in Christianity. Even though God can be known through his creation, this revelation is limited in comparison to what can be known of him from his self-revelation in history. And the only access later generations have to God's revelation in history and in Christ is through the witness to this history and to Jesus Christ found in the Bible.

The English word 'bible' is derived from a Greek word, *biblia*, which is the plural for 'books'. Consider the similar plural in the expression 'Holy Scriptures', which is also used for the Bible. This plural is appropriate, for the Christian Bible we find nowadays bound together in one volume is in fact a collection of books. There are sixty-six of these, which Protestants call 'canonical' books, to which Roman Catholics add a few more, called 'deuterocanonical' books. These books are divided into the Old Testament, which Christians have in common with Judaism, and the New Testament, which tells the story of Jesus and the first generation of his followers.

These sixty-six books were written over a significant period, of maybe up to 1,500 years, and use a great variety of styles. Some of the central texts are historical narratives: they tell the story of God's dealings with Abraham and his descendants, of Israel, of Jesus, and of the early church. These books witness to God's revelation in history. But the Bible does not consist only of historical narratives. It contains a great variety of other genres, including oracles of God, legal texts, prayers, poetry, proverbs and descriptions of visions and dreams.

All these texts reflect an important tension, which often amazes people who read the Bible for the first time. On the one hand, the Bible presents itself as the 'Word of God', and Christians believe that that is precisely what it is, because through the Bible God himself speaks to them. They believe that God's Spirit guided the authors of the Bible, so that their words would communicate God's own message. On the other hand, the Bible is a very human book, representing many different human voices, writers, styles and perspectives. To people who expect a book dictated by God, which is how, for example, the Qur'an presents itself, this doesn't add up easily. For Christians, this makes the Bible all the more realistic and all the more dear to them. The God of the Bible is not a God who is aloof from the mess of history; he has acted in the midst of it. The God of the Bible is not afraid of using limited human beings to share his word; rather he has made himself known to people with often limited cultural perspectives, but as such he speaks right into the midst of the world in which we live. The God of the Bible is not afraid of people asking him questions and even at times raging against him. All those voices can be found in the Bible. Rather, the God of the Bible takes people seriously with all their questions, doubts and emotions.

Christians call the Bible 'the Word of God', for it is through the Bible that God continues to speak to his church today. In an important sense, the whole movement of revelation reaches its goal only when God speaks to people today. This movement of revelation starts with God acting in history for the liberation of his people, and culminates in God becoming a human being in Jesus Christ. The movement of revelation also includes the proclamation of these events by the Old Testament prophets and New Testament apostles, who, in their proclamation, also explain what these events mean for humanity. Christians believe that in giving these interpretations, these prophets and apostles did not just give their personal opinions about what it all meant, but that they were guided or 'inspired' by the Spirit of God himself in their understanding of how God was revealing himself in this history. This process of God's self-revelation further includes the divine guidance and the selection and collection of the texts by the believing community into what became the Bible. Christians believe that the same Holy Spirit guides those who read the Bible today, showing them that this is indeed the Word of God which leads them to life in all its fullness.

2. The Identity of God

The greatness and closeness of God

One of the most characteristic features of the Christian faith lies in the way it balances a strong belief in the greatness of God on the one hand and his closeness to humanity on the other. By itself, this is a feature of many religious traditions. Philosophers may come up with a concept of a divine reality that occupies a realm entirely different from ours, but religions are interested in *relating* to this reality. Religions grow from the conviction that the relationship between humanity and this world of God, the gods, or the divine is of utmost importance. They seek to help people to relate to the divine. Most religions suppose at the same time that this divine reality is radically different from us and that we therefore need an – often elaborate – system that helps people to relate to the divine.

In the Christian faith we encounter the same tension in both sides of the relationship between God and humanity: his greatness and his closeness. The tension is in many ways stretched almost to breaking-point. In a well-known biblical passage (Isaiah 57:15), we read:

> *For this is what the high and exalted One says —*
> *he who lives forever, whose name is holy:*
> *'I live in a high and holy place,*
> *but also with those who are contrite and lowly in spirit,*
> *to revive the spirit of the lowly*
> *and to revive the heart of the contrite.'*

On the one hand, therefore, Christians put great stress on God's holiness. This is not an easy concept, but when we bring together a number of terms from both the Bible and the Christian tradition, we may find ourselves glimpsing something of this aspect of God. When Christians say that God is holy, they refer to the fact that he is different from reality as we know it. He is radically different in terms of his nature. God is the Maker of the universe and therefore entirely different from what he has made. God transcends the temporal, transient, finite world we see around us. God is infinite, eternal, all-powerful and all-knowing. He is self-sufficient and depends on no-one and nothing but himself. He is also holy in the moral sense: there is no evil in him, no obscurity, and he is therefore radically different from a world and humanity permeated by evil and sin. He transcends this world and exists in his realm of glory.

On the other hand, he is also a God who enters into a covenant relationship with humanity, who speaks to them through his prophets and through the Bible. He loves them to such an extent that he wants to enter into a relationship with them in which he is described as the Father, the Friend, the Lover and the Bridegroom of his people. Many biblical passages and images evoke a deep sense of tenderness and closeness. God became so close that he even lived among humankind in the person of Jesus of Nazareth, up to the point of sharing human life, joys, suffering, deceptions and even death.

This tension between God's holiness and his love provides Christians with a major challenge for their lives with God. There is a constant risk of stressing one side of the equation at the expense of the other. God easily becomes so holy and remote that it is hard to relate to him. This may have been the case in certain forms of medieval Christianity in which God's holiness and judgment were often vividly pictured. On the other hand, it is also possible to stress his closeness, his readiness to give and to forgive, so much that people forget about his holiness, his transcendence, how awesome it is that we can relate to this God. This may be the case in certain strands of modern Western Christianity, in which God sometimes becomes above all a super-daddy who is always there to support his children when they feel down and encourage them in their projects, but provides no radical challenge to the way they organize their lives.

God's holiness and transcendence of course have major implications for everything Christians can say about God. They realize that they can speak about God only in terms of the world they experience around them. When describing God as a Father, a Friend and a Lover, Christians are not saying that God is exactly like the fathers we encounter in day-to-day life. Christian thinkers would use the term 'analogy' here. God is similar to a father, but in a way which is appropriate to him; he relates to us in a manner that is analogous to how we relate to friends, but in a manner which is also different because he remains God. When Christians call God all-powerful and all-knowing, they start from a common understanding of power and knowledge, but realize that this applies only analogously to God: God knows in a way appropriate to his nature, which infinitely transcends human ways of knowing. Yet Christians believe that it is still appropriate to call God a friend and all-knowing. God remains in an important sense incomprehensible.

Christians believe that they can never understand him fully. Yet they believe that the knowledge they do have is adequate and true, for it originates in God himself, who wants to be known by human beings and has made himself known to them.

A personal relationship with God

A personal God or an impersonal 'ground of being'

The tension between human efforts to describe God in terms of analogies with the world around us and the realization that God remains always different are apparent in every description Christians use for God. This is also the case when Christians understand God as a person or as personal. When Christians say that God is a person, they mean that God acts towards human beings in a personal way, in a manner analogous to the personal relationships we encounter among human beings.

When Christians call God personal, they indicate that they believe that he is a God who acts, who loves and who communicates. God's creation of the universe was his own decision and act. He didn't have to create the world, and the fact that he did so was an expression of his love, of his free and loving choice to call this world into existence. When God acts in the history of the liberation of humanity, this is another deliberate choice on his part. He could also have left the world to itself, but the fact that he does act for the liberation of humans is also an expression of his love. When God communicates with them, this again rests on a free choice on his part to make himself known and to be known by humanity. When he became a human being to live among humankind, this was an expression of his personal love and desire to save humans and to come close to them. When he sends his Spirit to live in them, this is because he wants to be intimate with them and to have humans share in his own divine life and love.

The importance of this understanding of God becomes apparent when we contrast it with impersonal understandings of God, examples of which can be found in major strands of Hinduism and in a number of philosophical systems such as Platonism. If the divine were an impersonal 'ground of being', it would be the ground and origin of all that is, but not in the sense that the universe is a result of God's creative act. It is more like the overflowing of its infinite existence. This overflowing or 'emanation' of his being would not depend on a choice, but would be automatic and necessary. All that exists would be in a sense the result of his goodness, but it would be goodness in an impersonal sense, more like the way a river is good when it shares its gifts than the way a mother is good when she shares her love.

People would then also relate to God in the way they relate to impersonal realities. God himself would not be sensitive to human love. Loving God would be more like loving beauty, truth or goodness than like loving a friend. In that case you could not say that God takes a personal interest in people or listens to their prayers. Believers might still pray, but prayer would be more like a meditation on the spiritual ground of being and its importance to human life than like a personal dialogue in which people express their needs, hoping that there is a God listening to them.

When Christians call God a person and use personal terms and images for him, they realize that God remains very different from human beings. Christians do not think of God as being like a bearded old man living in some place in the universe called heaven. This is not just something that would be true of a limited circle of sophisticated Christians who choose to understand their religion more spiritually. An average Christian town-dweller or farmer in the first century after the birth of Christ would know that God fills the entire universe and beyond, and that calling God a King does not mean that he sits on a literal throne in heaven. The same is true for Christians with little formal education today, be they abstract-thinking Europeans, or Africans who tend to think about God in more concrete images.

When Christian artists pictured God as an old man sitting on a cloud, they did so knowing that God himself is spiritual and invisible. Yet, when Christians call God a person, they think they are saying something about God that is true. They say that personal images convey something essential about God that impersonal images can never capture. God is not just light and beauty; he is Father and King. Many Christians believe that images of personal relationships indicate in a deeper sense how we relate to God than images of impersonal relationships. Humans relate to God more as subjects relate to a king and as children relate to a father than as a drop relates to the ocean or a ray of light relates to the sun.

God as Father

One of the most personal titles Christians use for God is 'Father'. In the Old Testament God is already called the Father of his people, but the title became much more important and personal in the New Testament because of the central place it had in the self-understanding of Jesus. Jesus spoke Aramaic and in his mother tongue he addressed God as *Abba*. This is commonly held to be an expression of close intimacy, similar to our 'daddy'. Jesus' way of addressing God was so remarkable that the Aramaic expression *Abba* was preserved in the Greek New Testament.

This relationship between Jesus and God was entirely unique, but Jesus also invited his followers to address God in the same way, as a child addresses its father. Christians consider themselves children, daughters and sons of God. Yet Christians see their own relationship with God as different from that of Jesus. In chapter 5 we will explore the unique relationship between Jesus and his Father. Christians do not consider themselves children of God by nature, as Jesus is; rather, through Jesus they are adopted into the family of God and as such they have the privilege of addressing God as their Father.

For Christians this evokes a deep sense of wonder and intimacy: what a privilege for simple human beings to call the Creator of the universe their Father! What this means becomes tangible in the best-known Christian prayer (compare Matthew 6:9–13):

> *Our Father in heaven,*
> *hallowed be your name,*
> *your kingdom come,*
> *your will be done,*
> *on earth as in heaven.*
> *Give us today our daily bread.*
> *Forgive us our sins*
> *as we forgive those who sin against us.*
> *Lead us not in temptation*
> *but deliver us from evil.*
> *For the Kingdom, the power and the glory are yours*
> *now and forever. Amen.*

This is a prayer Jesus himself taught his followers. If Christians begin their prayer by addressing God as Father, they do so with great confidence that God listens, understands, cares and seeks the best for them. At the same time it expresses humility, the recognition that God is so much greater than human beings, and that although humans may not always understand God's dealings with their world and with their lives, can trust that God's plans are best. In his perfect wisdom he knows how he will bring about the coming of his kingdom, his reign, in the history of the world and in the individual lives of those who pray.

The belief that God is a Father evokes, however, not only feelings of trust and intimacy. For many women both within and outside the church it evokes images of male domination, and a number of feminist Christian thinkers have therefore argued that the expression is no longer appropriate for God. It reflects relationships in a patriarchal culture, where the power of men in general and of the patriarch in particular was backed up by the authority of God. Others, both men and women, find it very hard to relate to God as Father, because they have experienced neglect or even abuse from their human fathers.

In view of these questions and criticisms, it is important to clarify what Christians traditionally have and have not meant to say when they called God 'Father'. Firstly, calling God 'Father' does not mean that Christians consider God as male. Though the Bible has a very positive view of human sexuality, it is very careful not to talk about God in sexual terms. The God of the Bible does not have a female counterpart, as many other gods of the time had. Calling God Father indicates the relationship God has with us: in an important way God relates to us as a Father relates to his children.

Secondly, it is important to recognize that images of what fatherhood means are indeed significantly influenced by cultural ideals of what fathers should be, and by personal experiences of our own fathers (or lack of them). This also influences how Christians understand God as Father. In a modern Anglo-American context, fatherhood is understood in terms of understanding, love and encouragement, while fathers in traditional Latino cultures are expected to be much more authoritarian and distant. Images of God in both societies reflect these cultural differences. Christians would say, however, that one cannot model one's understanding of God's fatherhood on particular experiences of human fathers or even on particular cultural ideals of fatherhood. God's fatherhood should be understood in the light of who God is and of how God relates to humanity as his children. Human fathers should model their own calling as fathers on the fatherhood of God, rather than the other way around.

Finally, it is important to note that 'Father' is not the only way of describing God in the Bible and in the Christian tradition. In the Bible we also find images of God which evoke ideas of motherly care. God upholds and carries his people as a mother carries her baby (Isaiah 46:3). Jesus talks about his own desire for the return of Israel to God in terms of the longing of a mother hen who desires to gather her chicks under her wings (Matthew 23:37). On the other hand, the image of God as Father is equally balanced by the image of God as Judge, King and Master, who has an absolute authority over his subjects, and as the Potter who can do whatever he wants with the clay, his creation. These different images of God are needed to develop a full picture of God and of his relationship to humankind.

The one God

The one God and the many gods

In the contemporary religious context, the belief that God exists as a Trinity, as a tri-unity of one God in three persons, is probably one of the most distinctive features of the Christian faith, and we must therefore give it proper attention. How did Christians come to accept this, at first sight strange, belief? What does it actually tell us about God? And what impact does it have on the Christian understanding of life and the world? Before the belief in the tri-unity of God can be properly understood, however, one needs first to have a grasp of the importance of the belief in the oneness of God. Christians believe that God made himself known as the one and only God and Creator of the universe before he came to be understood as existing in three persons.

Christians share with Judaism this conviction that God is one, and inherited it from their common history of God's dealings with the people of Israel. The belief that there is only one true God was at the centre of Israel's religion and made it very different from those of the surrounding peoples. It placed the Jews and Christians together in a category that was radically different from the polytheism – the belief in many gods – that was so prevalent in the Roman Empire, where the earliest Christians proclaimed their message. Christians were even labelled as 'atheists', because they rejected the many gods of the surrounding peoples. How revolutionary this was becomes clear when we reflect for a moment on the way people relate to the gods in a polytheistic universe.

In a polytheistic universe, people do not need to reject someone else's religion. One simply accepts that there are many gods and that people have different gods. The fact that someone worships the gods of his region does not preclude one from fully recognizing the need for others to worship their gods. People can even maintain relationships with several divinities that have different roles for different needs and different areas of life. In those days in the Roman Empire, people believed in various types of divinities, to which they related differently. Firstly, there were the gods or spirits of the family, who protected the family and might be worshipped at a little altar in the house. Next, there were the gods of the city and of the region, which had particular power in a certain area, which protected the city and its people, and also represented the greatness of that city. On a third level, there were the gods of the Roman Empire, which represented the power of the state. It was all right if the conquered peoples continued to worship their own gods, as long as they also venerated the Roman gods and the statue of the emperor, representing the absolute authority of the empire over local gods and local interests. On a fourth level, there were personal gods that were venerated across the empire, gods with which people had a personal bond, from which they accepted special help and to which they might have sworn allegiance. These might have been gods brought into the empire by foreign peoples and that were experienced as particularly powerful or attractive, such as the Persian Mithras; but they might also be gods with which people developed a particular relationship because of their function, as with Asclepius, a god with healing powers.

This ancient polytheistic universe has a number of important parallels with certain movements and ideologies in the contemporary world. It obviously has parallels with polytheistic religions that exist today and with polytheistic tendencies in important strands of Hinduism. It has parallels with certain pluralistic interpretations of religious variety in today's world. Such pluralist thinkers would say that the different religions should not exclude one another, but rather consider them as religions that are most appropriate for a specific region or culture, with Hinduism being the religion for India, Islam for the Middle East and Christianity for Europe and the Americas. Alternatively, religious preferences may be thought of as personal choices relating to the ideals and lifestyles individuals find most attractive and most appropriate to their life projects.

Living in a one-God universe

In a monotheistic universe, a universe with only one God, the relationship with God is entirely different. As Paul Tillich, a twentieth-century American theologian originating from

Germany, pointed out: the difference between monotheism and polytheism is not just a mathematical difference concerning the number of gods. It is a qualitative difference with regard to how people relate to their gods. In the first place, if there is only one God, who is the Creator of the universe, everything that exists is made by him and there is, therefore, nothing beyond his control. His power is not limited to a certain family, city or region. This means that people can have absolute confidence in the one God and in his power to protect them, in contrast to a polytheistic universe, where people always needs to fear that the god of choice or of the community can encounter another god who is more powerful, and that their god might not be able to protect the city against the more powerful armies and gods of the enemy.

Secondly, if there is only one God, this means that there is a basic unity in life and in the universe. Human life is then not just a conglomerate of life experiences in different public spheres and relating to different private interests. That is what life might look like in the polytheistic world, and what it definitely looks like in the contemporary world, which lacks a sole centre and instead has multiple centres of interest and value: the state, the local community, science and economic powers in the public sphere, and in the private sphere love for the family, a link with a number of friends and places, a sense of beauty, a certain take on truth, a personal passion, a hobby, a small contribution to making the world a better place. In a monotheistic universe the world is not just made up of elements that are at worst warring against one another and at best indifferent to one another. Life is not just a patchwork of incoherent bits and pieces with a few threads that run through. The universe originates from a single source and develops towards a single goal, and all the elements in human life should find their meaning in relation to this one God, in relation to whom every aspect of it finds its true meaning.

If there is only one God, this means, thirdly, that people

cannot choose a god according to their own needs and liking. Rather, God chooses them. Religion is not about people using spiritual powers for their own projects, be it the glory of their nation or their personal success or self-fulfilment. Religion is about human beings accepting God's project for his world and trusting that their lives will flourish when they submit to a reality bigger than themselves. For Christians, true religion is not about human beings choosing to give a certain spiritual meaning to their lives; true religion is about finding the meaning which the one God and Creator has given to life.

In the fourth place, in a monotheistic universe where there is only one God, the Creator, nothing in this created world is divine. The Roman Empire can no longer claim divine authority and absolute allegiance by asking that its emperor be venerated as a god. If there is only one God, all human authorities are just that, human authorities and subject to criticism as needed. The Christian belief in one God implies a huge criticism of the tendencies seen in states and other human systems to make themselves absolute, be they Nazism, Communism or the more subtle self-absolutizing of free-market capitalism. Communism and capitalism may have provided useful tools for the organization of economic life in society, but they are never above criticism and can never become absolute values and goals in themselves.

The three-in-one God

Origins of belief in the tri-unity of God

The difference between Christianity and other monotheistic religions is thus not so much about the belief that there is only one God, who is the transcendent origin of the universe.

The difference rather has to do with how this unity should be understood. Muslims, for example, understand the oneness of God in an absolute sense, allowing for no differentiation whatsoever in the Godhead. Christians understand this unity rather as a unity of love between three persons in the one Godhead: the Father, the Son and the Holy Spirit.

The idea that there is only one God who exists in the unity of three persons is not easily grasped, and it took the Christian community a number of generations before they felt that they had come up with a satisfactory formulation of it. The church would not have arrived at this teaching had it not felt that it was the only way to understand the richness of God's self-revelation. Although the Bible itself does not explicitly relate the idea of the Trinity, this was the only concept by which to do justice to how God had revealed himself in Jesus of Nazareth and in the gift of his Holy Spirit to the church. In later chapters we will deal more fully with how Christians understand the identity of Jesus and of the Holy Spirit; here we will simply glance at a couple of pointers to their divinity.

The first followers of Jesus – also called 'disciples' – quickly realized that in Jesus they encountered much more than a great teacher or prophet. He did things only God can do: he taught with absolute authority, forgave sins, showed authority over nature in quieting storms and healing sickness, and called people to follow him. He claimed to be the saving presence of God himself that had been promised for so long. He demonstrated that he lived in an unprecedentedly close relationship with God his Father. And after his shameful execution on a cross, God brought him back to life, or rather gave him life in a higher degree and thereby affirmed Jesus' amazing message and work. God showed him to be the promised anointed King. No wonder people felt prompted to worship him. Rather than rejecting this worship, as a good devout Jew should do, Jesus accepted it, because he knew that he was no ordinary man, but that he shared in the life of God himself. Thus Christians continued to worship Jesus after he returned to God the Father, with whom he shares in the rule of the universe. They therefore encountered God not only as the transcendent Creator of the universe, but also as living among them in the person of Jesus the Christ.

After his resurrection, Jesus sent the Holy Spirit to guide and empower his followers for the task for which he had sent them into the world. The Holy Spirit was no new concept to these first Jewish followers. They had encountered the Spirit of God in their own Jewish Scriptures, in what Christians now call the Old Testament. There the Holy Spirit was God himself being active in the world. This Holy Spirit was now sent to fill the lives of the disciples of Jesus, and in the process they experienced the power and the personal presence of God in an entirely new way. Here they were confronted with a third presence of God: God was not only the Creator of the universe and present in Jesus of Nazareth, but also living in them as the Holy Spirit.

The first Christians were therefore confronted with the personal presence of the one God in two very specific ways in Jesus and in the Holy Spirit. And these, while being the presence of God himself, were at the same time distinct from God the Creator of the Universe: Jesus, though divine, prayed to God his Father; and the Holy Spirit was sent to live in the disciples as if they were his temple, helping them to worship God who at the same time remained the Creator upholding the universe.

Picturing the three-in-one God

There is no space here to explore the development of the belief in the tri-unity of God. It is sufficient to say that this belief grew out of the early Christians' remarkable experience of God.

Christians see it as the only way to make sense of God, who, in his self-revelation, showed himself to be (1) the Father and Creator of the universe, (2) the Son who lived among humanity as Jesus of Nazareth, and (3) the Holy Spirit who continues to live in the church. The church came to the conclusion that if this is how God reveals himself, this must also be what he is: one God existing in three persons; a real unity and a real threeness in one and the same God. It is of course not easy to picture this and to understand how it all fits together, but that does not mean that it does not make sense. As Augustine said: 'If we can understand it, it is not God.' Christians consider this an encounter with true mystery, with the depths of God, which humans cannot fathom. They do not regard this appeal to mystery as a cop-out to avoid having to explain something that simply does not make sense. (It is true, though, that the notion of mystery is often abused in this way.) Christians feel obliged to respect this reality of a three-in-one God rather than explain it away. As a broad parallel, Christian thinkers sometimes point to physical research into the nature of light, which from one perspective behaves like particles and from another behaves like waves. We cannot picture both aspects in one single image of what light is, but do need both models to do justice to the reality of light, and, in scientific calculations we can see how both can be true at the same time. If the physical world is as complex as that, the Creator might be expected to have infinitely more depth to his being.

Christians have used many images to explain the doctrine of the Trinity. It has, for example, been compared to the three leaves that make up one single shamrock, or to the ice, water and steam that are all forms of H_2O. The fourth-century theologian Augustine compared it to will, memory and intelligence, which together make up the single human mind. Another group of early-church theologians, the so-called Cappadocian fathers, compared the Trinity with three different human persons who still share the same human nature. All those analogies are simply images and all fall short, because they either stress the threeness (three leaves, three human persons) at the expense of the oneness or, vice versa, the oneness (one mind, or the same substance, water, which appears in different forms) at the expense of the threeness. It is not entirely strange that nothing in the created universe adequately mirrors how threeness and oneness can go together in God. Yet some human experiences can provide important hints. One such experience may be that, in some of the most worthwhile loving relationships, people can experience a growing unity, which nevertheless does not diminish the difference of the other, but in the unity of love rather affirms the otherness. In the same way, Christians think of love as the essence of God's being and both the source of unity and relationship in God.

The love of God at the origin of the universe

I have stressed that Christians realize that no human being would of himself have come up with this mind-blowing idea that God is three in one. They believe it arose because this is how God showed himself to be. Once Christians had discovered that God is like this, it has appeared, however, to be an extremely rich idea. It has major implications for how Christians see life, and solves a number of riddles that confront not only Christians, but also others who believe in one God.

The belief in the doctrine of the Trinity has major implications for the Christian understanding of life. If God is triune, it means that he lived from eternity as a loving community of three persons. Love is essential to who he is, and he created the world not only to express his creativity, but to share his love with humanity, which is at the centre of his creation project.

The Trinity also explains something more about the personality of God. There are other religions that believe in a personal God, but it is difficult to imagine how God could be personal independent of the existence of the universe to which he relates. Personhood seems to presuppose relationship, so how can God be personal if he is absolutely one? The belief in the Trinity explains how: the one God exists from eternity as a loving community.

For Christians, personhood, relationship and love are therefore not by-products of a blind evolutionary process, by-products destined to destruction when the universe is extinguished or collapses into a gigantic black hole. Nor are they ephemeral and transitory in a religious universe centred on an impersonal divine reality to which humans can relate only by extinguishing their selfhood. Human beings are rather called to reflect the love and community of God in loving relationships and communities, and the temporary relationships people enjoy in this world are meant to find their fulfilment in the eternal love affair between God and humanity in which the triune God will invite them in the eternal circle of his love. We will explore this in more detail later when we discuss Christian beliefs about what it means to be human (chapter 4).

The Trinity also gives a deeper insight into the tension with which we started this chapter, between the greatness and transcendence of God and his closeness to the universe. Both in philosophical thinking and in religious life, there has been a tendency to stress one side at the expense of the other. Philosophically the infinite metaphysical distance between God and the physical world may be developed, and religiously the holiness of God may be stressed, at the expense of his desire for an intimate relationship with individual human beings and with humanity as a whole. On the other hand, his nearness may be stressed at the expense of his holiness and transcendence.

Understandably, it has been difficult to hold both aspects in balance. If God is truly transcendent, sufficient in himself, how could he be intimate with humanity? On the other hand, if God desires to enter into a loving relationship with humankind, would that not imply that he is in some sense in need of humanity and therefore not truly transcendent?

The doctrine of the Trinity gives an insight into how this can be resolved. God exists as an eternal community of love. He is self-sufficient and in no need of anyone else in order to experience the full extent of love. Yet, precisely because he is this eternal circle of love, he is able to share his love with a creation which he made precisely because he wanted to share this love. The closest parallel may be the love of a husband and wife who need nothing but the love of each other for the fulfilment of their relationship. Yet their love may flow over into a desire to share this love with children, whom they welcome into the circle of their love. Because they have each other, they do not depend on the love of their children and can therefore love them freely and unconditionally. Similarly, God, who is an eternal community of love, can open this circle and create a universe in order to lavish his love on it and especially on humanity as the crown and goal of his creation.

3. God the Creator

One of the fundamental questions of life is how we relate to the universe in which we find ourselves. Is this vastly expanding universe fundamentally indifferent to the existence of humankind, as modern materialist and evolutionist understandings would have it? It had, after all, existed for billons of years before *homo sapiens* appeared on the scene, and it expands billions of light years beyond our tiny Earth, solar system and galaxy. Is it even the case that this universe is hostile and humankind needs to chisel out an existence in an absurd and chaotic environment in which the extinction of our race is a constant danger? Is the world around us fundamentally an illusion, as taught in strands of Buddhism and Hinduism, and should we therefore look for what is ultimately real in a world beyond? Or are we part of a pantheistic universe in which the divine permeates all, and in which we will find our true identity when we realize that we are part of this encompassing unity of being?

The Christian answer to this question is found in the belief that the universe is the gift of God the Creator. One of the old Christian confessions of faith, the so-called Apostolic Creed, starts with this important belief: 'I believe in God the Father Almighty, Maker of heaven and earth.' The fact that this statement comes at the very beginning of the creed indicates that none of what follows, none of the other principal Christian beliefs, can be properly understood without understanding what it means that the universe originated in the loving choice of God, who wants it to exist and wants it to be what it is.

Like the other answers to the question 'How do we relate to the universe in which we find ourselves?', the Christian answer has major implications for how Christians understand and experience their lives. In this chapter, we will therefore explore not only what Christians intend to express by this belief in creation, but also what that means for the Christian understanding of life in the world. We will also explore the closely related idea of 'providence', which says that as Creator, God is not just the origin of the universe, but continues to be intimately involved with it. He continues to take care of it and guides it into the future for which he created it in the first place.

Creation

Creation from nothing

When Christians understand the universe as the creation of God, they take this to mean that the universe has its origin in a free act of God. There was a time when the universe did not yet exist. There was nothing but the trinitarian God, who chose to create this universe. This central feature of the Christian belief in creation is relatively easy to grasp, but at the same time has far-reaching consequences. If the universe exists, because God chose for it to exist, it could also not have existed. That of course underlines the frailty of human existence, but also makes clear that existence is a gift to the universe and to humankind, because God wanted it to be so.

This wonder about the gift of life resembles the discovery of a child who for the first time in her life realizes that she could very easily not have existed if her parents had never met, had no or fewer children, or had decided on an abortion. At the same time the child may realize that her parents wanted her to exist, that her existence is no accident, but rather a gift from her parents, who want the child to be part of their life. Life is an amazing gift. Christians believe that this creativity of parents who can bring new life into the world reflects in a dim way the creativity of the Creator God, who called the whole universe into existence because he wanted it to exist, out of his love.

Order and chaos

Before the creation of the universe, nothing existed except God, and therefore Christians have understood creation to be 'out of nothing'. God started from scratch, even more so than when a meal is started from scratch, for he literally had nothing to begin with. This may seem a rather abstract idea, but its importance becomes clear when we compare it with other understandings of the origin of the world that were current when the Bible was written. The peoples surrounding Israel and among which the Christian church came into existence had their own stories about the origin of the world. We would now call them myths: they tell stories about how the gods were born, about mythical battles between the gods, and between the gods and the powers of chaos.

As myths, they were not just stories told to pass the time, but expressed foundational convictions about the nature of reality. According to these myths, the gods were not eternal. They were themselves born or came into existence out of primeval matter and they therefore had no absolute power over the world around them, because they found themselves in a universe which had its existence independently of them. Their powers were limited by these forces of 'chaos' (the unordered original matter), by the existence of other gods, and above all by the overarching power of 'fate' that determined all that happened. The creation of the world and of human existence was therefore a battle against the powers of chaos. The 'cosmos', the structures of our world, existed in constant conflict with these chaotic forces. Human beings were not at home in the world; rather, their existence was profoundly threatened.

In the Jewish and Christian understanding, God was not limited by any pre-existent matter when he created the universe. He could therefore create it entirely to his liking. Thus he has complete control over the universe, control that is limited by nothing beyond himself. Humankind can make the universe its home, for God created it to be its habitat. As we will see in the next chapter, Christians believe that God tasked humankind with making the earth habitable, with cultivating it and becoming creative developers of culture. The earth was not ready-made, but was created precisely for this goal, and as such it welcomes humanity. From a Christian perspective humankind is not living in a fundamentally hostile world.

This is not to say that Christians deny the reality of chaos. It is so easy to understand that people came to such conclusions, particularly in these ancient cultures when life was so much more fragile and the world beyond control. Yet from a Christian perspective, this universe is not by nature, by itself, chaotic. It has become chaotic because humankind did not live as its Creator wanted it to live, because of what Christians call sin. Sin has not only made human society chaotic, hostile and dangerous; it has also had a major effect on creation as a whole, which shares in some way in the disastrous downfall of the human race.

In the next chapter, we will explore further how Christians understand sin, but for the moment we can already see an important implication of this for how Christians live in this world. God has given human beings freedom to organize their lives in this world. He has accepted the consequences of the fact that they chose not to live the good life God wanted for them, when they chose not to live in relationship with him and in submission to him. He accepted that life in the world became chaotic because of this. But this is not the last word. Chaos is not the final reality of this world, and God is in no way limited by the mess humans made of it. Christians believe that people have reason to entrust themselves to this God. Nothing is beyond his control and they can trust that he is able to bring this universe to the goal he intended for it.

Creation for a purpose

An important part of the Christian understanding of creation is that God did indeed create it with a view to a goal. Given that God could have chosen not to create this universe, one would suppose that he had reasons when he did so. In the Christian tradition different answers have been given to the question of why God created this world.

A first answer is that God created the world 'for his own glory'. The world exists to the glory and for the honour of the Creator. The beauty of the universe is a tribute to the greatness of its Maker, and humankind is created to express the greatness of God in recognizing him, thanking him and singing his praises.

If this were the only answer, we might think God had selfish motives in creating the world. It might even seem as though God were vain and liked to be pleased by his tiny creatures.

There is, however, a second answer to the question of why God created the universe. He did so in order that humankind might live in a loving relationship with him. He created it out of love and out of his desire to share his love with humankind.

This second answer is not as opposed to the first as it may seem. The seventeenth-century Westminster Shorter Catechism, a summary of faith in the Reformed tradition, brings both together. In answer to the question 'What is the chief end of man?' it answers: 'To glorify God and to enjoy him forever.' When people praise something, they enjoy it, and the better the object of their praise, the greater their enjoyment is. One may praise and enjoy a good meal, and the better the chef, the higher the praise and the richer the joy. Yet our praise and enjoyment of a beautiful work of art, of friendship or of a deep love surpasses by a long way our praise of a good meal. Christians often call on one another to praise and worship God. This is not because they serve a selfish and vain God, but because God is the highest and most beautiful reality and the love of God is the best they can ever enjoy. Praising him shows that people have discovered what is most beautiful and most worth living for.

This enjoyment of God by his creatures may be reciprocal. Christians think of God as being an abundance of dynamic creativity and joy. Maybe God simply enjoys creating a beautiful universe in the way an artist enjoys expressing herself in a work of art; maybe God takes pleasure in sharing his love and creativity in seeing human beings love one another, love him and express their own creativity when they create something beautiful in this world.

There is another important answer to the question about the purpose of creation. Though not all would share this perspective, an important group of Christian thinkers have said that the universe was created for Jesus Christ. When God became a human being in Jesus of Nazareth, he did so in order to save the world. Yet this was not the only reason. He also did so because he wanted to come as close to humanity as possible, because he desired human beings to know him as intimately as possible, not for himself, but so that humans might enjoy this closeness and intimacy. This closeness was not only a new possibility for the people who met Jesus of Nazareth physically in first-century Palestine. Christians of later ages also relate to God through Jesus of Nazareth, whom they encounter when they hear about him and read about him in the Bible. Even more, Christians believe that Jesus Christ is still alive and present today through his Holy Spirit and that they will one day meet him face to face. According to this view, God created the world for Jesus Christ; that is, with the purpose of sharing himself with humanity by sharing human existence in Jesus.

Creation and evolution

In this context, we may need to say a few things about the relationship between Christian belief in creation and the scientific theory of evolution. Since the development of the theory of evolution in the nineteenth century, there has been significant tension between both approaches to the origin of the universe. In the understanding of many, the theory that the universe and life gradually evolved has discredited the idea that God is the Creator of the universe. Given that many consider that the theory of evolution is proven beyond doubt, this places the Christian faith in a difficult position in the modern academic world.

Christian thinkers have reacted in different ways to this challenge. Some have provided an alternative explanation to the scientific discoveries that have led to the development of the theory of evolution. As such we find, particularly in North America, Christian centres devoted to so-called 'creation science'. These defend the idea that the universe is relatively young and that it came into being over a short period, possibly as short as the six days mentioned in the Bible. They are convinced that these beliefs can still be held in the light of recent scientific discoveries and that they might even be the best explanation of the data.

Other Christian thinkers have entirely accepted the current theory of the evolution of the universe and have said that the Bible stories about the creation of the world tell us something completely different about the universe. Like other ancient myths, they do not intend to give a literal description of reality that could compete with a scientific picture of the world. Rather, they tell of how one should live in this world and relate to it.

A third group steers what they see as a middle course that tries to do justice to what is valid in the two other approaches. They would recognize that the biblical stories about the creation of the world are not meant to be read as scientific texts. Yet, in their own particular language, these biblical stories tell us something true about the world in which we live, which is the same world that is described by the theory of evolution. We need to ask how both pictures of the world relate to each other. These Christians believe that the biblical message of the creation stories is that the whole universe has its origin in God, but that they do not necessarily provide a theory of how the universe developed. The biblical stories use their own literary means to convey this truth. Modern scientific study of the universe does indeed reveal many indications that this universe has existed for billions of years and has gradually developed. Modern science, however, does not recognize its own limitations, when it expands the scientific theory of evolution into the ideology of *evolutionism*. Evolutionism does not just say that the world has gradually evolved, but also that this is all there is; there is nothing more to be said about the world and about humanity than that they are products of blind evolution and chance. In response, Christians would say that the gradual development of the universe and of life could well be the means God has used for his project of creation, but that this tells us nothing about the ultimate origin and meaning of the universe. They suggest that current scientific theories may even give important indications that evolution is not the final word and the only reality, but that this evolving universe may have its origin in a higher reality.

In certain respects it is easier to be a scientist and a Christian now than a hundred years ago. Firstly, the theory of the 'Big Bang' proposes that the universe evolved from a giant explosion around 14 million years ago. This idea of an evolving universe seems to be reconcilable with the Christian idea that the universe is not eternal, but has an origin in time and in God, wherever this moment might be located. A number of both Christian and non-Christian thinkers have furthermore argued that the universe shows many signs of 'design'. It does not give the impression of being a random event, but rather suggests that it has evolved following a precise and well-designed plan. This again points to the existence of a Designer, whom Christians would identify as God. The debates have not yet reached their conclusion, but many Christian thinkers and scientists experience recent developments in science much more as an exciting invitation to explore how their faith relates to science than as a threat to their personal faith.

Living in a God-given world

It must be clear by now that the belief in creation has major implications for how Christians understand their life in this world. It means that life and the world should first of all be received as a marvellous gift. That is why the expression of thanks to the Creator is so important for Christians. Many Christians 'say grace' before every meal. This term is shorthand for a prayer in which they express their gratefulness for the gifts of God. At mealtimes these are most tangible in the gift of food, but at the same time saying grace articulates gratefulness for the gift of life itself.

Belief in creation also means that what humankind receives from God is fundamentally good. It may not be good as it is now, because of the destructive influence of sin, because of what humankind has done with these good gifts. People have, for example, used the natural resources of the earth to make weapons for destruction rather than tools for the betterment of life. They have used the gift of language as a means to deceive others rather than as a tool to build and enjoy relationships. They have used the gift of sexuality to exploit others rather than to celebrate committed and faithful relationships. Yet none of these gifts is wrong in itself, and the Christian message is therefore always fundamentally positive. So often, Christians are perceived as being against so many things, being the killjoys of wider society. The belief in creation is one of the elements that should help to show that the Christian message – and also the Christian moral message – is essentially positive: God has given humanity life and a good world in which they may live. They may enjoy it to the full. Morality, rather than being a killjoy, is a guide to living life in its fullness so that it may flourish in all its aspects.

Yet, though Christians see this world and life in it as good, it is not the final and ultimate reality and in that sense they live in a world which is different from that of the materialist and evolutionist. They believe that life receives its meaning and purpose from its relationship with the trinitarian God, who created it. This does not make the world less real, as in Eastern perspectives which have stressed the transience of reality, and have even called it an illusion that pulls people away from their true identity, which can be found only when they detach themselves from this world. Christians believe that they are called to live in this world, but in relation with the Creator. In the next chapter, we will explore this further.

Knowing the delicacy of this balance between living in this world, but with an orientation beyond it, the Christian can easily understand why people can be tempted to take up such contrasting views as either the Buddhist perspective or the secular one. Apart from its Creator, this world does indeed seem to have a fleeting and transitory nature, which means that human beings can never find ultimate rest in it. Add the reality of profound suffering that seems an unavoidable part of life in this world, and it is easy to understand why people search for a home in the world beyond. On the other hand, this creation is radically different from the Creator. Christians do not believe that we live in a pantheistic world where the divine penetrates everything. In such a world people can be so caught up in the life of the here and now that the Creator can be easily forgotten. Hence the possibility that people live their lives as if God did not exist.

Providence

Providence and prayer

The Christian belief in creation is closely related to the notion of the providence of God. By the term 'providence', Christian thinkers have indicated several different things. At the most basic level, it means that God did not leave the created universe to itself, but continues to uphold it and take care of it. It furthermore indicates that God knows what will happen in the future. The idea goes further, however, than simply knowing the future. It also means that God is guiding history and bringing it to its intended goal. How Christians understand that goal will (appropriately) be dealt with in the last chapter of this book, which discusses the end of history. Finally, Christians also use the notion of providence to talk about God's special care for them personally. They believe that God is intimately involved with every individual one of them.

This last aspect of providence is of course most visible in the Christian practice of prayer. Christian prayer has many different aspects. One of the most important of them is what they call 'petitionary prayer': they express their needs and their petitions to God. They ask God to help them, in guiding them in their lives, in taking care of their needs and in protecting them from all harm. They pray not just for themselves but also for those whom they love and even for the whole world.

For people who are not religious, this practice often seems rather bemusing and even bewildering. How can Christians pray to God to help them when the world seems to run pretty much its own course, propelled by the laws of nature and other processes which we may not understand but which seem to show little evidence of any divine involvement? And how can Christians so earnestly thank God when life goes well, when half the time it turns out differently? It all seems quite childish and a flight from the harsh reality that we earthlings have to figure it out for ourselves in this world.

These questions are actually shared by a number of Christians themselves, particularly by Western Christians. Christians from non-Western cultural backgrounds often find it easier to see God at work in their lives, and they therefore tend to pray more often, more earnestly and about many more aspects of their lives. This may have to do with the affluence of many Western Christians, who experience less need for God in many aspects of their daily lives. It is also related to the fact that Western Christians have been profoundly influenced by the same secular and scientific understanding of the world that makes petitionary prayer so bewildering to many non-Christians: life seems to be governed by laws of nature that leave little room for God.

Providence and the laws of nature

Christian thinkers have realized, however, that the regular processes of nature do not contradict the idea of divine providence. Rather, they have their place in a wider understanding of God's relation with creation and with humanity. To begin with, the regularities of nature are themselves part of the beneficent provision of the Creator. He created the universe in such a way that there would be seasons according to which people can organize their lives; so that there would be plants that produce seeds that can be sown; so that there are natural materials that have certain properties that can be used to make tools; so that there are certain laws of nature that give things their order and expected behaviour.

It is only in such a world that humankind can take care of itself in providing for the future. It is only in such a world that humankind can express its creativity, create cultural products and artwork, and develop this world. It is only in such a world that humankind can be responsible for its actions. God created a world with natural laws as a provision for humankind and so that humankind could at the same time participate in meeting its own needs. There is therefore no contradiction between God's gracious provision and human responsibility to provide for the future. God does not take care of humankind as a parent takes care of a baby or toddler, but rather as a parent provides for a growing child who needs to learn to be responsible, including when that means accepting the consequences of irresponsible behaviour.

Christian thinkers such as the Cambridge scientist-theologian John Polkinghorne have also pointed out that natural laws do not function in such a way as to leave no room for flexibility at all. This rigid understanding of scientific laws dates from the Early Modern Era (around the seventeenth century) and has been corrected by more recent scientific developments such as those associated with quantum mechanics. Rather natural laws describe regularities that leave space for other influences. One of these is of course the role of human actors: human life is not entirely determined by natural laws. People's experience indicates that within the world of regularities they have a certain scope of freedom and that their choices amount to something.

Polkinghorne adds that this world of regularities also leaves scope for a God who acts. The regularities of the natural order do not unfold independently of God, but rather should be seen as processes upheld by God that express his continuous care and fidelity to what he has made. God is not bound by them, but actually upholds and guides them intimately for the good of humanity and for the good of creation as a whole. If it is true, as Christians believe, that this God is a personal God who relates to each human being personally, then it makes sense to pray and to ask God to act on their behalf. When Christians pray, God can show them what to do and guide them to make the right choices. God can also prompt others, and maybe especially other Christians, to act on his behalf and to work for the good of people around them or for the good of people with needs in distant countries. He can also guide natural processes in such a way as to accomplish particular goals. Christians experience the action of God on their behalf in miracles, but also in events that others might explain as lucky coincidences. As one person said: 'There are just too many coincidences in my life; that cannot be coincidental.' Like miracles, such events may cause amazement and gratefulness to God, even though it might be possible to explain them in other ways.

According to traditional Christian belief, God will also sometimes intervene in the ordinary course of things and do something which goes entirely against the normal laws of nature. The resurrection of Jesus Christ from the dead would be the primary example. Christians know that dead people normally don't come back to life again, and they see this as a specific intervention of God. Most Christians believe that God does sometimes still act in this way and that he still performs miracles. Some would point to the stories of miraculous healings at Lourdes, and others to Pentecostal healing services. Some of these might involve the healing of 'psychosomatic' illnesses in which God works through natural processes. Other healings might be interventions in which God acts more spectacularly in contravention of the laws of nature.

Providence and Jesus Christ

Christians themselves do not always find it easy to believe in the providence of God. This is not only a modern phenomenon. In the Bible itself we encounter complaints of believers who felt that God had forgotten them. They may have been experiencing deep suffering, which was sometimes aggravated by the fact that others who did not care about God seemed much better off in life. The biblical figure of Job is a proverbial example. It is remarkable that such experiences and complaints are recorded in the Christian Scriptures. It reveals that these Scriptures have never downplayed the reality of suffering and evil. So, Christians of other times can learn from their own Scriptures. People who are tormented by their sufferings are sometimes given answers that are much too easy and slick, as if their suffering was not that serious. The Bible does, however, take suffering utterly seriously and describes God as a God who is willing to listen to the complaints of tormented people.

Part of the answer to this experience of suffering would entail a reference to sin: God has allowed humankind to reject him, and to steer its own course with all the terrible consequences that this has brought and still brings. The Christian understanding of sin and evil will be explored further in the next chapter. Yet, though the reality of sin may explain the existence of suffering, it does not always provide an answer to the specific suffering Christians experience in their own lives They may ask: 'If God takes care of every individual human being, if he is intimately involved in every aspect of my life and if he is in control and can avert evil, why do I have to experience this particularly intense suffering, which seems so far beyond my fair share and which is more than I can bear?' When such questions come up, Christians often look to what they learn about God through Jesus Christ. As we saw in our discussion of revelation (chapter 1), Christians believe that what they can learn about God from his general dealings with the world is fairly limited in scope. In order to know God's deepest intentions and in order to know God's plan, Christians look at his special revelation, particularly in Jesus Christ. The way God acts and reveals himself in Jesus Christ deepens the Christian understanding of God's providence in important ways.

First of all, Christians learn through Jesus Christ what God aims for in his providence. God's primary aim is not that we should live easy and agreeable lives. According to Christians he has a much greater project for us: he desires people to come to know him and develop a loving relationship with him. God gives *himself* to humankind and that is far greater than everything else. Experience shows that people who live easy lives often have little interest in anything that goes beyond the mere pleasures of life. In his providential dealings with his people, God is luring them on so that they may start looking for something that is far greater.

Secondly, Christians learn through Jesus Christ that God's project with individual human beings is not limited to their own short lifespan. Christians see the resurrection of Jesus Christ from the dead as a sure promise that there is a life beyond death, a life in God's eternal kingdom in a renewed universe (see chapter 8). In Christ, God has shown that he is capable of conquering death. From Christ, Christians learn that they should not measure the worth of their lives in terms of what this life has to offer. This life is just the prelude to something much bigger to come. Someone who enters a tough boot camp measures its value only in the light of what comes next (compare Romans 8:18).

When they look to Jesus Christ, Christians learn, in the third place, that God can bring good out of the most dreadful evil. When Christians reflect on Jesus Christ dying on the cross, they see someone who seemed utterly abandoned by God. Yet, three days later, Jesus was raised from the dead and it became clear that God had not forsaken him. What is more, Christians believe that when Jesus Christ died on the cross, God was acting in a mysterious way for the salvation of humanity. It was not just his own suffering that he bore, but in a way he bore the sin and suffering of the entire world. In doing so, Jesus opened a new way to life right through this suffering and his victory over it. In chapter 5 we will come back to this, but here it is important to note that this has important implications for the Christian understanding of God's providence. It shows that God does not abandon his people in the deepest suffering, but that he brings good out of suffering and evil. And it shows that God can be completely trusted when people entrust themselves to him, just as Jesus did.

Finally, Christians see in the suffering of Jesus Christ the supreme proof of God's love for humanity. They believe that in Jesus we encounter God himself. If Jesus is God who had taken up human existence, it means that God knows what suffering is. He is not a faraway God who watches people suffer from the safety of his remote heaven. Rather, he loves them so much that he was ready to accept this suffering for their sake. That is why they believe that whatever happens in life, nothing can separate them from the love of God that he has shown in Christ (Romans 8:35, 38–39). This love is more precious to them than anything else. When one thinks of how much people are ready to suffer for the love of a woman or a man, one may begin to understand what this much greater love is worth.

4. Humankind as the Distorted Image of God

The paradox of human existence

What does it mean to be human? And what is the meaning of my own existence? These questions have preoccupied many ordinary people who struggle to make sense of their lives. Even the wisest and most intelligent people have found them hard to answer, because human existence seems such a paradox. The seventeenth-century French philosopher Blaise Pascal explored many of the paradoxes of human life and characterized the human being as a 'thinking reed'. On the one hand human beings have incredible capacities. As thinkers, they explore the remotest regions of the universe. They reflect on the origins of the universe and on its future. Their minds can encompass millions of years and billions of light-years. Their desire to know does not limit itself even to space and time. The Bible says that God 'has set eternity in the human heart' (Ecclesiastes 3:11). In the Christian tradition this has been understood as a reference to the desire in the human heart to know the eternal God.

Humankind has these great capacities and aspirations. Yet on the other hand, humans beings are just a 'thinking reed'. A passer-by can crush it or snap it off without a thought. Human life is so fleeting and fragile; entire peoples and generations have gone by, hardly leaving a trace. This fragility becomes even more tangible when people we love pass away; we see a unique, irreplaceable life cut off in its bloom or slowly withering away.

The contrast is not just between the ephemeral nature of life in the history of the universe and our desire to have a lasting significance. There is a more shocking paradox between our high moral ideals and our unsurpassed capacity for hatred and destruction. Humankind could produce both Hitler and Mother Theresa, Pol Pot and Gandhi. It is disturbing that high ideals and shocking moral failures exist together in the same people. Many cannot live up to the ideals they set themselves, and the best human institutions seem to have dark and oppressive sides to them. States that have fought for freedom can oppress minorities. Capitalist economies that have generated unprecedented wealth have done so at the expense of the poor elsewhere and have produced their own type of poverty: a scarcity of real community and meaningful relationships.

In the light of these paradoxes, it is not surprising that different thinkers and movements have come up with opposing explanations of the riddle of human existence. The most contradictory views can gain some plausibility by drawing on a narrow band of human experience. At one end of the spectrum some Buddhists say that the whole material world and all human relationships are only an illusion. What is real is *nirvana*, to which people can aspire when they turn away from the world in meditation. At the other end we find those who tell us that only what we can touch and see is real. The human being is nothing but the highest primate, and religion is only a flight from reality. At one end we find those who say that human beings are essentially individuals and that they can build relationships only when their individual identity is firmly established. At the other end we find those for whom the individual exists only as part of the collective and for the collective, be it the clan in which they are born or the totalitarian state to which they belong. Many other contradictory perspectives on what it means to be human could be mentioned.

The Christian faith has its own answer to the riddle of human existence. It is an answer that tries to do justice to both sides of some of the central paradoxes of human existence. It regards human beings as essentially related to God, yet places them squarely in this world in which they are called to live with this God. It sees them as made for life in community, yet as being individually responsible before God. It recognizes how humankind is enslaved to self-destructive lifestyles, yet it does not give up the ideal: the belief that life can be lived differently, and better, following God's blueprint for human existence.

In the rest of this chapter we will explore this Christian answer to what it means to be human. We will first look into the belief that human beings are the 'image of God', which is the central Christian concept for God's project for human life, what he intended for our existence. Next, we will examine what Christians believe to be the origin of evil and destruction in the world: sin. In the final section we will investigate the role of Jesus Christ in the restoration of the marred image of God in humankind.

Created in the image of God

The focus of God's attention

As we saw in the last chapter, Christians understand the whole universe as God's creation. This implies that everything in the universe exists as a consequence of God's love and that God created everything with a purpose, with a plan in mind. Within this plan for the universe, human beings have a central place. According to the biblical creation story, human beings were created as God's latest and most special creature.

Since the rise of modern science, it has become profoundly counterintuitive to say that humankind is at the centre of creation. We may experience ourselves as the centre of our small worlds, but it seems childish to suppose that this corresponds to reality. In the long history of the universe, *homo sapiens* is an extremely recent arrival. In its vast expanse, the Earth on which we live is an almost infinitesimally small speck. Yet Christians believe that God created the whole universe with special regard to humankind, for whom he has a special plan. God is like a writer who has produced a thick volume just in order to build up to this one phrase in which he expresses his deepest thoughts. God is like the lover who prepares for months and even years, and travels long distances, in order to utter that one short phrase: 'I love you, do you love me?'

Unexpectedly, more recent discoveries about the nature of the universe have made it less strange to believe that humanity is at its centre. Physicists speak about the 'anthropic principle', by which they mean that the universe from its very beginning has evolved in a manner which makes life possible. If the universe began with a Big Bang, maybe 14 billion years ago, it gained many of its crucial characteristics in the first milliseconds of its existence. Many of the physical constants that were determined at that early stage were fine-tuned in a way that made it possible, billions of years later, for life to come into being. Maybe this is a hint by the Creator about the special plan he has for humanity.

If this is a hint, even a strong hint, it can be no more than a hint which accentuates the riddle of human existence. The universe remains silent on why humans have this special place, or what precisely God's plan is. Here we need what we have called 'special revelation', and it is there that Christians look for an answer (see chapter 1). In the Christian tradition, the central beliefs about what it means to be human have been expressed by the notion that humanity is 'made in the image of God'. This expression is used in the Bible in the creation story, when human beings appear on the scene for the first time.

The term 'image of God' tells us first of all that in the whole of creation, humankind has a special relationship with God: only humans are created in God's image. It also points to the fact that they were created for community: they were made in order that they might flourish in developing deep relationships with others around them. The expression also points to a special relationship with the rest of creation, which humans are called to care for and develop creatively, mirroring the Creator. In the next three sections we will look at these three relationships, which are, according to Christians, central to what it means to be human: our relationships with the non-human creation, with our fellow human beings, and with God. The expression finally points to the fact that humankind is meant to find its ultimate fulfilment in relationship with Jesus Christ. He is the image of God in a unique sense. We will return to this special role of Jesus at the end of the chapter.

Creation and culture

In the creation accounts in the opening chapters of the Bible, our attention is particularly drawn to the relationship between the human beings and the wider creation. In the first creation story we read: 'So God created human beings in his own image. […] God blessed them and said to them, 'Be fruitful and increase in number; fill the earth and subdue it. Rule over the fish in the sea and the birds in the sky and over every living creature that moves on the ground' (Genesis 1:27–28). This blessing can therefore be understood as a consequence of humanity being created in the image of God. When the Bible was written, people were used to seeing images of gods and of kings. These statues represented the authority of these gods and kings over the cities where they were placed. The Bible considers humankind in similar terms as the image of God. Humanity has received the authority of God over creation, to take care of the world and to subdue it.

In the Christian tradition, this part of the story has been labelled 'the cultural mandate'. God has given humankind a mandate for the development of culture. In this context, culture should be understood in a wider sense as everything that humans do with nature in order to make it a place where they can live and where life is good. Culture in this sense includes the tools with which human beings till the ground and domesticate animals, the technical developments that give them an increasing mastery over their environment, the language that allows them to communicate and make sense out of their world, and the social structures that are developed to organize their communities. In the history of humankind, we encounter a mind-boggling variety of cultural expressions and an amazing technical inventiveness on the part of peoples living in environments ranging from the Arctic to the rainforest. We see the greatness of the mind expressed in art and literature. Christians see this as part of what it means to be created in the image of God. As his image, humans are called and equipped to mirror some of God's creativity and resourcefulness.

This element of the creation story has always been an aspect of the Christian tradition, but it has received particular attention since the sixteenth century. Through the development of science and technology, people became increasingly aware of the power they had over creation and recognized this as an authority given by God. This authority could, however, easily be abused. We have increasingly seen how humankind's special position has become a pretext for exploiting creation. The depletion of natural resources, the extinction of thousands of species, widespread pollution, and global warming, all confront us with the disastrous consequences of this exploitation.

This exploitation of the earth's resources rests, however, on a misinterpretation of the cultural mandate and an abuse of the authority given to humanity. As the image of God, humankind is called rather to be the steward of creation by taking care of it and by developing its potential. This is explicit in the second of the creation stories told in Genesis, where the first man, Adam, is placed in the Garden of Eden, which represents the earth as a whole, given to humankind. He was placed there 'to work it and take care of it' (Genesis 2:15). In the face of the destruction of the environment in the twentieth and early twenty-first centuries, Christians have become increasingly aware that we need to be more serious about this 'taking care' of the earth. Human beings have no absolute authority over creation, but are only stewards. They are accountable to God for what they do with it. As his image, they should reflect his love and care for the world.

Created for community

Humanity as the 'image of God' is called not only to be God's steward on the earth, but also to live in relationship with fellow human beings. The first creation story stresses that the Creator created human beings 'male and female' (Genesis 1:27). This has been understood to mean that in their existence human beings are fundamentally open to and in need of others like them. One sees this especially in the need of the first man, Adam, for a companion, whom God gave him in Eve, the first woman.

God's creation of humankind as male and female does not necessarily mean that everyone must be married or at least experience sexual love in order to be fully human. In the New Testament and in the later history of the church, the celibate lifestyle has been respected as a way of life in which our human potential can also be fully developed. How could Christians say otherwise when Jesus himself lived a celibate life? It does, however, mean that humans can flourish only when they live in relationships of friendship, affection and intimacy with other people around them. This Christian understanding of what it means to be human reflects a deep human reality that we need other people. An example can be found in Nelson Mandela's experience on Robben Island. In his autobiography he tells about all sorts of punishments and humiliations he and his fellow political prisoners had to suffer under the apartheid regime. Yet none of them was so hard and so dehumanizing as the long periods of solitary confinement. This deprived them of one of their most basic human needs: company. Many others who, for whatever reason, have been unable to develop healthy relationships with those around them would strongly resonate with this.

The Christian understanding of human beings as created for community contrasts with the individualism which is so characteristic of modern Western culture and which the West is currently exporting to other parts of the globe. According to fundamental strands of Western thought, communities are based on contracts between people, who are first of all considered as individuals. Society as a whole is seen as founded on a 'social contract'. The idea is also reflected in contemporary approaches to the relationships of married couples and of people who live together in non-marital relationships. This individualistic perspective implies that in order to enter healthy relationships, one first needs to be able to function as an independent individual, so that one does not run the risk of creating unhealthy dependencies. A consequence is that these relationships are primarily evaluated in terms of the benefit they bring to each participating individual. From a Christian perspective, however, the goal of human existence is not to become a self-sufficient individual. Persons become healthy individuals only in relationship. It is only in community and in being affirmed and challenged by others that individuals become what they are meant to be and that they can fully flourish.

In this respect the Christian faith contrasts not only with modern individualism, but also with Buddhism. Buddhism promotes showing mercy towards those in need and in that way demonstrates a strong interest in the community. Salvation, however, remains a very individualistic concept: the Buddhist searches for personal enlightenment, and attachment to others is seen as an obstacle to such enlightenment. Such attachment leads to suffering, but subsequently also keeps one from what is truly important: one's gradual disentanglement from society and from the world in order to seek fulfilment in *nirvana*, the eternal bliss in which all personal existence and consciousness will be sublimated. Christians recognize the fact that relationships often lead to suffering, but when the people who are most dear to us cause us to suffer, Christians know that this reflects the importance of such relationships for human existence. They see in those imperfect and often painful relationships a reflection of the relationship with God that surpasses all human relationships. In relationship with God, people find true fulfilment, but not in a manner that disengages them from their communities and from those dear to them. The fact that they find their fulfilment in God, who can never fail, should rather help them to live in true friendship and deep love with those who so often fail them and whom they so often fail.

It is precisely as a community that humankind is the image of God: they are called to reflect the community that God is in himself. As we saw, Christians see God himself as existing in an eternal loving relationship of three persons – Father, Son and Spirit – truly one in love, yet truly different as Father, Son and Spirit. Humankind can dimly reflect this divine mystery of love when people discover that they become more truly themselves, more truly individual, more truly personal, when they love others and know they are loved by them.

Created for a relationship with God

In the last two sections, we noted that the Christian understanding of human beings as the 'image of God' implies that they exercise authority and stewardship over the rest of creation and are called to live in community. But we must not miss the obvious point that the term 'image of God' defines human beings primarily in terms of a special relationship with God. It is as 'image of *God*' that humanity has these special callings. Christians believe that human beings were created to have a special relationship with God. This primary calling is expressed in what Christians call the 'great commandment', the central ethical principle that should guide the Christian life: 'Love the Lord your God with all your heart and with all your soul and with all your strength' (Deuteronomy 6:5). In more contemporary language: 'You should love the Lord your God with all you have and are.'

According to Jesus, this calling to love God is even more important than what is called the second commandment: 'Love your neighbour as yourself' (Matthew 22:39). This priority of God is related to the greater claim God has on human lives: he is their Creator and King. It is also related to the unsurpassable value he has for them. Augustine argued perceptively that people should measure their love according to the value of what they love. Chocolate is great, but when I love it more than I love my children, I should reconsider my priorities. We should always love our fellow human beings more than any material gift: they are unique and irreplaceable. Christians believe that we should love God even more. They believe that God loves humans and offers himself to them, so that they may enter into a loving relationship with him. The value of this relationship obviously surpasses everything in the created world, even the people and communities that are most precious to them.

This is why the biblical commandment to love one's neighbour is balanced by other biblical exhortations that people should be willing to leave their father, mother, spouse and children, those who are most dear to them, for the sake of God and for the sake of Christ (Matthew 10:37). If their relationships and communities keep them from loving God, they should be made aware of where a Christian's priorities lie. This may seem harsh, but Christians believe that human relationships become unhealthy when people try to usurp the place of God and claim absolute authority over others. They become equally unhealthy when people look to other human beings to fulfil their deepest needs, which only God can fill. Putting God first may therefore in the end have a healthy effect on other relationships.

This shows why Christianity is opposed not only to modern individualism, but also to different forms of collectivism or totalitarianism in which the individual is suffocated by the needs of the community. In the Bible and in history we encounter many instances of individuals standing up in the name of Christ against totalitarian regimes and against the totalitarian claims of their smaller communities. They knew that their first allegiance was to God and that in choosing God they were simply placing the highest value on what is most valuable. Christians who stood up against the Roman Emperor, communist regimes and other totalitarian claims have been a constant reminder that such regimes overstep their authority when they claim absolute allegiance.

For Christians, their understanding that they are made in the image of God is therefore not some abstract, speculative or mystic idea bearing little relation to day-to-day life. It has major ethical implications about what they should value and what they should value most. It implies a conviction about how human life can flourish and, conversely, what ways of life are destructive. It explains why materialism will never satisfy if people chase after career and material possessions at the expense of their relationship with family and friends. It explains why people can find no ultimate satisfaction in life when they keep God out of the picture. As Augustine famously said, addressing God: 'You made us for yourself and our heart is restless until it finds rest in you.' At the beginning of his autobiography Augustine used this phrase to characterize his life. He wasn't a Christian then and didn't yet know the love of God for him. But with hindsight he concluded that all the restlessness, all the deep longing, which he experienced in his life was caused by the fact that God had created him in order that he might know God. That is why nothing else could ultimately satisfy Augustine.

Sin and its destructive consequences

Sin as missing the goal

The Christian idea that God created human beings for a purpose – to live in a loving relationship with him and the people around them and to reflect his care and creativity in their cultural expressions – is the crucial background for understanding the closely related idea of sin. The Christian idea of sin is easily misunderstood. Many would understand sin primarily as the transgression of some divinely set law: God has given his commandments and punishes us when we disobey. In many people's minds this evokes the image of a king who imposes his authority by dictating arbitrary laws. Such a God is easily perceived as a killjoy, a God who especially forbids those things that are most fun – such as sex outside marriage.

Christian language can easily give this impression when it talks about divine rules, laws and commandments. And indeed, because he is Creator and King of the universe, Christians would wholeheartedly agree that God has this authority to tell humanity how to live. Yet, when Christians submit to this authority, they do not experience God's rules as arbitrary. If God created human beings for a purpose, he gave them his laws to ensure that they wouldn't miss this marvellous destiny he set for them. Sin is the transgression of God's law, but that law is not arbitrary. Rather, it expresses God's great plans for human existence and for his universe.

Christians sometimes explain the idea of sin by using the concept of 'alienation'. When people sin, when they do not live according to God's calling for their lives, they are alienated from their true beings. That is why they will at times be deeply dissatisfied with the way they live. So often, they have the feeling that they are not living up to their full potential, that there should be more to life than they are currently experiencing.

This sense of dissatisfaction is often masked by the projects people have for their lives. They think everything will be fine when they finally reach their goal: 'I'll be satisfied when I've bought that house or got a better job, when I'm in a relationship, when I have children…'. But after they have achieved their goal, the restlessness remains, and they may set themselves further goals without pausing to ask themselves whether they are setting the right goals. Christians would say that many of the goals we set ourselves, or that the world around us sets for us, alienate us from our true selves, our true destination. These goals may not necessarily be evil in themselves. It is normal to seek recognition and an adequate income. It becomes problematic, however, when people develop an inordinate desire for fame, power, or material wealth, pursuing these things at the expense of relationships that they should value more: with the people that are closest to them and, supremely, with God.

Because sin alienates humans from what they are meant to be, it is also destructive. Here we see again how God's laws are not arbitrary, but are given so that life may flourish. Consider one of the so-called Ten Commandments: 'You shall not give false testimony against your neighbour', or, more generally, 'It is not good to lie about people.' Why isn't it good? Because only people who trust each other can form healthy communities. Where people constantly need to be on their guard to check whether people are holding things back or cheating, they cannot flourish. Maybe they can develop self-reliance in such a setting, but they cannot develop the type of relationships that make life worth living, relationships of mutual trust and true friendship.

We have seen how a distorted relationship with the environment similarly leads to exploitation and self-destructive patterns of behaviour. Christians would say that similar patterns can be seen in people's relationship with God. They believe that if we do not give God the right place in our lives, we are not living up to our full potential. And what is more: we set in train destructive patterns of behaviour, because we try to replace God by what can never replace him; we try to fill the void in our lives that only God can fill. That is what Christians call idolatry: replacing the true God with another god or simply with something else that isn't God. People either entrust their lives to someone who is ultimately trustworthy or they entrust themselves to something or someone that will finally fail them. They either look for fulfilment of their deepest desires where it can be found, or they look somewhere where they can only find surrogate fulfilment that will finally leave them empty.

Sin as slavery

The fact that sin is inherently destructive leads us to another closely related characteristic of sin: sin enslaves. According to Christians, sin cannot just be understood in terms of wrong deeds. It is not as if all people need is to be told how to behave properly so that they can then behave better and live as they are meant to live. Christians have found that the destructive patterns of behaviour in their lives are often stronger than they are themselves, and they share this experience with many others.

Christians point to different levels on which sin enslaves human beings and makes them prisoners of forces that are stronger than their own determination to live differently. They see this first of all at the level of debasing and destructive habits that become stronger and stronger and steadily gain a firmer grip on people. Drinking to excess is an obvious example, and many people wish they could change their smoking and eating habits, but find this very difficult. We can find similar patterns in other areas of life, though they may be a little less obvious. People may come to understand that dishonesty undermines their relationships with the people closest to them, but they keep falling back, and each each time they do that they become more entangled in deceit: they need to tell increasingly complex lies to keep up with the virtual reality they have begun to spin around them. People may decide to make more space for friends in their lives, but old habits of making the wrong choices keep creeping up on them.

What makes these old habits so entrenched is not just that they are individual patterns of behaviour. Our habits are enforced by our cultures, societies and communities. As individuals, we may decide to eat more healthily, but find ourselves bombarded by advertising for all kinds of food, whether it is good for us or not. And the marketing people know how to make us want what they think we should want. As individuals, we may decide to spend more time with our families, but the pressures of work may make it very hard to follow through with these good resolutions. The scope people have to give a greater place to God in their lives is also determined, largely by their cultural context. Is their life entirely absorbed in those parts of our secularized society where God is almost completely marginalized? Do they encounter Christians who make God their central focus and live attractive lives, or do they only encounter religious people who make life with God seem rather unattractive?

Christians believe that sin is engrained not only in habits and in social relationships, but also in people's thinking, particularly in the dominant thought forms of societies. The Christian picture of what makes life worth living and what makes communities flourish, sketched above, differs from the dominant values of the societies in which we live, be they Western or non-Western. These societies bombard people with their preferred images of the successful life as exemplified in their idols. These ideas can easily absorb its members, and their omnipresence can make the weirdest ideas sound plausible. For example, some people end up believing that a high bank balance will make someone happy, or that it is intolerant to share deep religious convictions with non-believers. This is a final way in which sin enslaves humanity: it infiltrates and obscures the human mind so that people have a hard time recognizing what is really true and really good.

Christians may stress different aspects of the way sin enslaves humankind. Some point to the way people's individual behaviour enslaves them and how they need to be freed from themselves. They place a lot of stress on the need to change one's personal lifestyle and to develop a strong Christian character. Other Christians have a sharper eye for sin in social structures and cultural values, and will point to the need for political liberation and the formation of a Christian counter-culture. These perspectives are not mutually exclusive; sin imprisons us at all these levels.

In this respect Christians differ from most Muslims and others who conceive of sin primarily in terms of doing wrong. For Muslims, sins are primarily acts of disobedience to God's good commandments. That is why God sent his prophets to call humanity back to his commandments and to the right way to live. That is why obedience and law are so central to Islam. Christians would agree that humans do indeed need prophets to call them back to God, but would want to say that they need much more: they also need a Saviour who liberates them from the enslaving power of sin. A prophet is not enough; his words, good as they may be, cannot by themselves save people from the enslavement to sin in which they find themselves. That is one of the reasons why Christians find it hard to accept Muhammad as the seal of the prophets, as a further prophet in the same line as Jesus. For Christians, Jesus is not just a prophet who teaches them how to live. He is also the Saviour, and when they consider how sin enslaves humanity, they can see no hope apart from Jesus' redeeming humans from the slavery of sin.

Original sin

The Christian idea that the reality of sin is much bigger than individual immoral acts is expressed in the term 'original sin'. This belief expresses the idea that sin is an all-pervasive reality. From the time when sin originally entered the universe (hence 'original sin'), no person living has been able to escape its reality. Everyone is born into a sinful world, and everyone living is therefore automatically contaminated right from the start (another connotation of the expression 'original sin').

According to Augustine, 'nothing is so easy to point out, nothing is so difficult to understand' as original sin. He definitely has a point there. The fact that sin is all-pervasive is confirmed daily. When we look at babies, we see perfect little bundles that we can only love, but as they grow they soon give evidence of different sides to them. Many people have had utopian ideas of building new societies free from the evil that pervades the world. Small groups have set out together to start new idealistic communities. Whole nations have tried to reorganize themselves according to utopian blueprints, as exemplified in the communist states. These societies have lived out some of their ideals and have kept alive the hope of a better world. Yet they have all succumbed to their own forms of evil, their own authoritarianisms, their own forms of exploitation, sometimes more overt, sometimes more covert, yet equally real.

Although it's fairly easy to point to the reality of original sin, it's hard to understand how it works. Why is sin is so pervasive and powerful? In the course of history, theologians have offered different explanations. In the Roman Catholic tradition, the tendency has been to understand original sin in terms of a natural unity of the human race. When Adam and Eve, the first human couple, sinned, their human nature was marred by sin, and this deformed human nature was subsequently inherited by all their descendants.

In the Protestant tradition, and particularly in the Reformed strand within it, the unity of the human race was understood as what was called a 'federal unity' or 'covenantal unity'. God had initiated a covenant with the human race and had appointed Adam and Eve as the federal head of this race. Just as the actions of a president on behalf of a nation have consequences for the whole nation the president represents, the sin of Adam and Eve had consequences for the whole community which they represented before God.

Recent developments in biology and cultural anthropology have suggested a new way in which one may understand 'original sin'. They have pointed out that human existence is profoundly cultural. Compared with other animals, human beings are entirely helpless when they are born. They cannot survive by their instinct and physical attributes – they have no claws, no speed, no protection. They can survive only when they have learned from their community how to cope with the world, and they can attain full humanity only when they are socialized within a community, learning its way of life and survival. They are therefore profoundly dependent on their communities, for better or worse. This may help Christians understand the reality of inherited sinfulness as a consequence of our being deeply social and cultural beings: because people depend on their communities when growing up, they inherit all that is good in their way of life, but also all that is destructive.

This new way of understanding original sin also helps to explain why God may have permitted sin to be hereditary. Why did God make the world in such a way that the sins of our

A Pocket Guide to Christian Belief

ancestors have disastrous consequences for their descendants? Isn't that unfair? No, if the fact that they inherit their sinfulness is only a side-effect of one of the most beautiful aspects of what it means to be human – the fact that humans are created for community, and are radically dependent on others if they are to flourish. And it is a consequence of their ability to develop culture as a reflection of the creativity of their Creator, each generation playing its part in creating the world into which the next generation is born. Children can only work with what their parents hand over to them, both the great gifts they share with them, and also the vain or even destructive habits, ideas and social structures in which they were educated.

The Christian understanding of evil

This rather gloomy picture of the human condition might suggest that Christians have a depressing outlook on life. Although some Christians might look as though they have such an attitude to life, most Christians would not agree that all is doom and gloom. The fact is that everyone needs to give some account of evil in the world, and Christians would want to argue that their picture is not only the most realistic but also one of the most positive accounts that have been given.

Let us consider some alternative understandings of evil. In the early centuries of the church, Christianity had strong competition from various kinds of Gnosticism. Gnosticism represented a very negative attitude to the world and to history. According to Gnostics, the whole physical world, including our bodily existence in history, is inherently evil. Being inherently evil, it cannot be redeemed. Gnosticism therefore proposed avenues for salvation that involved a flight from the world; a liberation from this bodily and worldly existence. Christian thinkers disagreed strongly: according to them, this world is indeed corrupted by sin, but it was created good, and is the object of God's redemptive love and of his work of salvation. Salvation doesn't mean flight from this world, but hope for the world, for the renewal and redemption of people's bodily existence, for their families, communities and nations. This hope contrasted sharply with the Gnostic idea that only individual souls can be saved, and this can only happen when they are finally liberated from their earthly confinement.

At the other end of the spectrum we find modern Western understandings of life which at first sight seem much more positive. Where Gnosticism rejected the whole of bodily and earthly existence as inherently evil, most modern Westerners tend to embrace it in all its physicality. There is a great appreciation of all the joys of our bodily and material existence. This is a very optimistic outlook on life, an optimism that may also be shared by other worldviews that have different ideas of what should be pursued, be it knowledge, love or justice. The general characteristic of optimistic worldviews is that they consider life as fundamentally good and as something that should be embraced. The evils the world contains can be overcome by understanding and education. When people discover what is good for them, they will automatically shun evil and want to follow the course of life proposed for them.

These optimistic and pessimistic outlooks on life described so far share a sense of good and evil. However, when people are thoroughly secularized, their consciousness of sin and evil may be virtually absent, and secularism constitutes a third basic attitude towards evil. It is hard to make sense of the notion of evil in an evolutionistic universe in which human behaviour is simply determined by the fight for survival of our genes, which are inherently selfish and need to be so if they want to survive.

Most outlooks on life can be classified as more or less radical varieties of these three basic patterns: basic pessimism, fundamental optimism, or the denial that the notions of good and evil apply to reality at its most fundamental level. Against the backdrop of these three outlooks on life, it becomes clear why Christianity, for all its recognition of the profound influence of evil, is fundamentally a message of hope. Christians would want to ask whether existence without clear moral notions of good and evil is really attractive. In an evolutionistic and morally indifferent universe, we can no longer condemn things as radically evil. Yet can we really say that the repulsion we feel when we encounter the Holocaust, the Rwandan genocide or a case of child abuse is simply a delusion? Is this just how the world is? It is possible that the experience of moral indignation is too strong and too central to one's self-understanding to write it off like this. If our indignation were nothing more than discomfort or distaste or an expression of our genes' desire for survival, the world would become a pretty bleak place. We would just have to accept that what we experience as evil is an unavoidable and morally neutral byproduct of evolution.

Basic optimism doesn't seem to offer a solution either. It is certainly more attractive, but is it realistic? Christians would claim that the notions of sin and of original sin are much more realistic in our world where evil is so pervasive and persistent. That is why, for all its gloominess, the idea of basic pessimism continues to impose itself. Societies may be optimistic for prolonged periods, but in periods of war and recession people realize that even during their best periods their optimism wasn't always justified and that it was possible only at the expense of denying the presence of evil. Some people have a basically optimistic attitude towards life, but relationship breakdown, death or some other disaster may make them think that fundamental pessimism has a lot going for it: even when they were at their most upbeat, it was often at the expense of denying the darker sides of their own lives and of shielding themselves from the deep suffering around them or in the rest of the world.

Against this background, Christians would claim that the biblical understanding of evil is deeply attractive. Rather than fleeing from reality, it realistically recognizes the pervasiveness, power and destructiveness of evil. Yet it sees evil not as a necessary and unavoidable characteristic of our existence, but as a consequence of human sin. And it provides hope in pointing to Jesus Christ, who is presented as the solution to evil, as the promise of a better world and as an invitation and empowerment to live radically changed lives – if, of course, the hope presented in Christ is well-founded and not a chimera.

Restoring the image

The inverted image

The sketch we have given shows that the Christian understanding of what it means to be human combines two starkly contrasting perspectives. On the one hand it provides us with a very high view: as the image of God, humankind is called to represent God's creativity and care for this earth; it is called to an intimate relationship with God himself, and to reflect the love of God in developing loving and caring communities. In sharp contrast, the doctrine of sin points out that humanity, far from living out this ideal, lives in alienation from its true being and has become enslaved to destructive habits and powers. This contrast makes up the riddle of the human condition with which we opened this chapter.

The radical distortion of the image of God by sin raises the question whether this distortion has gone so far that it no longer makes sense to call human beings, in their sinful and fallen state, the image of God. This has provoked vigorous debate between different theological traditions. From the second century AD onwards, theologians such as Irenaeus of Lyons have made a distinction between the 'image of God' and the 'likeness of God'. According to Irenaeus, the 'likeness' of God has been lost through sin: human beings no longer reflect the love of God in their lives. The 'image' of God has, however, remained intact: humans are still rational and moral beings. These characteristics distinguish them from the other animals, cause them to be like God in certain respects, and make it possible for them to be restored to the likeness of God through the saving work of Jesus Christ and the Holy Spirit.

Protestant theologians, beginning with the sixteenth-century Reformer Martin Luther, have been much more pessimistic. According to Luther, the image of God is so deeply marred by sin that it is almost entirely lost. Humankind's rational and moral capacities have not remained intact, but have been corrupted by sin, and made to serve self-centred desires and projects.

Both of these positions can draw on certain ideas in the Christian Scriptures. On the one hand we find passages which suppose that even in a sinful world, the human being should still be treated as the image of God. It is because every human being is created in the image of God that murder is strictly forbidden (Genesis 9:6). On the other hand we also encounter the idea that human beings need to be restored to the image of God and Christ, suggesting that this image has been lost or at least severely distorted by sin (Romans 8:29; Colossians 3:10). Both positions can also draw on human experience. It seems right to say that no human faculty and no area of human behaviour have been spared by the destructive influence of sin. But still there seems to be a qualitative difference between humanity and the rest of creation. Most people recognize that murdering a fellow human being is in a different category than killing an animal.

Many contemporary theologians would therefore say that both these perspectives on the image of God have something valid to contribute to a balanced Christian understanding of what it means to be created as the image of God. There is something that makes human beings different from other animals, and that something is related to their high calling to be a mirror of the love and creativity of God in this world. Yet, when people are not living according to that calling, the image is marred and distorted. It may actually be more accurate to say that the image is inverted. It is not that the image is diminished: human beings still have a deep need for God and for their fellow human beings; they still have a great capacity to rule over creation, to develop culture and to build societies. Yet these needs and capacities have become inverted. People try to satisfy their deep desire for God in other ways, seeking what can never fully satisfy. The need for fellow human beings is equally inverted in a desire to manipulate and control others for selfish needs. The capacity to rule over the earth has become exploitative rather than caring. The image of God has been deeply corrupted, but even in its corruption it reflects the special place of humankind in the world. Even the most inhuman behaviour shows this, for the fact that it is done by human beings is precisely what makes it so repulsive.

Renewal in the image of Jesus Christ

In the last section we looked at an important contrast between Roman Catholic and Protestant theology in their teaching about the image of God. A third tradition, Eastern Orthodox theology, brings its own perspective to the wider debate over what this concept means. The Orthodox tradition tends to understand human beings less in terms of their past creation and more in terms of their future as the image of God. Orthodox thinkers point to the fact that Jesus Christ is also called the image of God. He shows in a unique way what God is like. Jesus Christ reveals the love and glory of God as never before.

In this Orthodox perspective, the understanding of the image becomes much more forward-looking: among all creatures on the Earth, human beings are the only ones that are called to become like Christ, the Son of God. Orthodox Christians in that context speak of 'deification' or 'divinization'. This does not mean that humans can become divine or a part of God. We should remember that Christians hold that there is an absolute difference in being between the eternal Creator God and the world he created. It does, however, mean that human beings are invited to share the divine life of love that God as Father, Son and Spirit is in himself. In that sense, the notion of the image of God does not only look back to creation. It also looks forward to a future, to a destination which far surpasses the humble origins of human beings as simple creatures. They are invited to enter into an incorruptible life, the eternal community which God is in himself, and thus 'participate in the divine nature' (2 Peter 1:4). These reflections lead us naturally into our next chapter, in which we will consider how, according to Christians, Jesus Christ restores humankind to what it was meant to be and brings it to its destination.

5. Jesus Christ and the Salvation of the World

The arrival of the reign of God

It is only in this fifth chapter that we arrive at the most crucial characteristic of the Christian faith, its most central belief: the conviction that God made himself known when he acted for the salvation of humanity in the history of Jesus Christ. You don't need to look far to discover that the Christian faith in its many expressions is all about him. That is why we have found ourselves referring to Jesus long before arriving at this point. We saw how the enormous variety of expressions of the Christian faith results from the impact of this one person, Jesus of Nazareth. We saw how Christians consider him to be the decisive self-revelation of God and see him as crucial to their understanding of both the greatness and the misery of humankind. It is at this point that we will explore the basic Christian beliefs about Jesus Christ in more depth. Here many of the shorter and sometimes enigmatic references to Jesus in the earlier chapters may gain a much fuller meaning than they had before.

At the same time, we need the background of the earlier chapters in order to grasp what Christians believe about Jesus and why he is so central to their lives and communities. The person of Jesus can only be understood against the background of the Jewish and Christian belief in a God who is the Creator of the universe, who is utterly distinct from this universe yet deeply committed to it and to its future. We can see his full significance only against the background of the Christian view of the human condition as alienated from its true being as the image of God and as subject to the enslaving power of sin. Only against the background of God's project for humankind, which he has been working out through the ages in the history of the people of Israel, can we fully understand who Jesus is.

God's vision for Israel

Christians share with Jews the conviction that God is working out his project over the course of history. He created humankind to be his image, to represent him in this world. Because of the failure of humankind to live up to this expectation, he chose Abraham and Israel, with whom he entered into a special covenant relationship. They were to be his special people, called to demonstrate to the world what it means to be truly human. As such, they were called to be the vanguard, the small beginning, of God's project for the salvation of the whole of humanity. They were the people of God who recognized God as their Lord and King, and as the King of the whole creation. They were called to show what it means when humankind accepts the reign of God and lives in obedience to his plans for them.

Yet, like humankind in general, Israel also failed to live up to God's expectations and purposes for his people and for humanity. There were, however, always prophets who called Israel back to these ideals, to live as a community that worshipped its Creator wholeheartedly and that lived together in peace and justice. There was always a small group of Jews who took notice of what the prophets were saying. The prophets considered this group to be the true Israel, those who were living out the special calling of Israel, in distinction from those who were Israelites in name but did not live up to their calling from God.

Increasingly, it became clear that the salvation of the world could not be expected to come from Israel or even from this faithful group within Israel. Yet the prophets received visions and messages that showed that God was not going to leave Israel on its own. One day, God would come to act decisively for the salvation of his people and for the salvation of the world. He would send the Messiah, the anointed King, who would liberate his people from all the oppressive forces that hindered them from living as the true Israel, the true people of God. He would send his Holy Spirit, who would be his personal renewing presence among his people. Thus he would change his people from the inside out. He would change their hearts, their inner beings, so that they would truly want to live up to their calling, and heartily embrace God's reign and commandments. And so they would be able to have an impact on the peoples around them and bring them to serve the God of Israel, who was the Creator of all.

Christians believe that these promises of the coming of the Messiah and of the gift of the Holy Spirit were fulfilled in Jesus of Nazareth.

The proclamation of the reign of God

The New Testament relates that Jesus of Nazareth was from the very beginning of his life unique. His birth was announced by angels, and was extraordinary in that he had only a mother and no human father. He was conceived by the direct intervention of God, which showed his unique nature and the unique role he was going to have. This is what is meant when Christians talk about the 'virgin birth' of Jesus. In antiquity, stories about miraculous births were relatively common, but to modern Westerners they are hard to take at face value. Many, including a number of Christian thinkers, see these stories as later mythical developments that underline the special role of Jesus but are not meant to be taken literally. Other Christian thinkers would, however, regard the miraculous birth of Jesus as entirely fitting when considered in the light of who he later showed himself to be. If he is the Son and the embodied message of God living among humankind, if he is the one who conquered the power of sin and death, if he is the one in whom God starts a new chapter with his creation, then these Christians argue that it is only fitting that he should enter the world not as an ordinary human being, but in a manner that reveals his unique origin and nature.

Yet, after his conception and birth, Jesus probably grew up as a fairly ordinary human child in his home village of Nazareth. As a teenager and young adult he may have followed the career path of his adoptive father, Joseph the carpenter. So when, at the age of thirty, Jesus began the life of a wandering preacher, people knew little of his origin and had a hard time figuring out who he was. In these early days, what struck people most of all was his message about the kingdom of God. This phrase, which is so common in Christian language, does not mean that Jesus came to establish an empire, beginning from first-century Palestine. The English word 'kingdom' is a clumsy translation of a term which refers rather to the 'reign' or 'kingship' of God. In the light of the earlier prophetic message to Israel, Jesus was announcing that the promises about God acting in history for the redemption of humankind, showing his power and forming a new people who obey him wholeheartedly, were about to be fulfilled.

Jesus was not just saying, however, that what many people had been waiting for was now going to happen. He was also saying that it was happening in a manner that was radically different from what many people expected. Among the Jews at the time there were different expectations about how God would come to liberate his people. Some were expecting a Messiah who would wage war against the empires that had oppressed Israel. The Messiah would be king in the style of the ancient heroic King David. He would crush Israel's enemies and reign over them in an era of unprecedented peace and prosperity. This would also ensure that Israel lived as the true people of God according to the commandments they had received at Mount Sinai. Others, however, were expecting an even more cataclysmic end of history in which the earth, sun, moon and stars would burn up and God would establish an entirely new universe.

In contrast to both of these visions, Jesus said that, initially, the reign of God would be inaugurated in a much more unobtrusive manner. This became particularly clear through the parables told as one of his principal means of communication. Parables are stories taken from everyday life to explain the nature of the reign of God. In one of them, Jesus compares the reign of God to seed that is sown. Sometimes the seed falls on stony ground and does nothing; sometimes it falls between thorns and thistles, and, though it sprouts, it is soon suffocated; only some of it falls on fertile ground, where it bears much fruit. In the same way, the message of the reign of God has different effects in different people's lives. In other parables Jesus compares the reign of God to yeast, which, when mixed into dough, does its work invisibly; and to a mustard seed, one of the smallest of seeds, which grows into an enormous tree. The reign of God in the current phase of history is hardly visible to those not looking for it, but it is present, changes lives and impels the world towards the goal of its history.

The identity of the King

The presence of the reign of God

Christians believe that Jesus has a very special relationship with the reign of God. He was different from the prophets who announced its coming. He was even different from John the Baptist, a prophet who was Jesus' immediate predecessor and announced that the kingdom of God was on the brink of entering the world. Jesus was not just announcing that the kingdom of God had finally come. In Jesus himself that kingdom was present. Through him, the reign of God becomes a reality, and wherever he is, God himself is at work for the salvation of his people.

This special role of Jesus became visible in his miraculous healing ministry. From the very beginning of his public activity, Jesus healed the sick, and that was of course a major attraction. People from all over the country brought their sick and handicapped friends and relatives to Jesus and he healed them. This was not just a way of showing off his power or of attracting people to listen to him. The consequence was rather the opposite of that; many people were so focused on his healings that they had little time to listen to his true message. Yet they were an essential part of what Jesus was all about. This is clear from the sermon setting out his mission, which he gave in his home town of Nazareth. When he was asked to speak to a religious gathering in the synagogue, he read this passage from the prophet Isaiah (see Luke 4:18–21):

'The Spirit of the Lord is on me,
because he has anointed me
to proclaim good news to the poor.
He has sent me to proclaim freedom for the prisoners
and recovery of sight for the blind,
to set the oppressed free,
to proclaim the year of the Lord's favour.'

Then he [Jesus] rolled up the scroll… He began by saying to
them, 'Today this scripture is fulfilled in your hearing.'

Jesus was claiming here that as he healed people, he was showing that the time had arrived when God was coming to liberate his people from illness, from oppression and from all the forces that hindered them from fully living and flourishing as the people of God.

To modern Westerners, this whole healing business seems to come from a different world. In a Western worldview, governed by the dictates of science, there is little place for miraculous healing. Christians would want to claim that here the scientific worldview shows its limitations. Science is an incredibly valuable tool for understanding the world as it normally functions. It is less capable of saying what can and what cannot happen. It is not capable of showing what God can and cannot do. If God is indeed the Creator of the world, he is also able to put right the things in the world that have gone wrong because of the destructive influence of sin. That is precisely what was happening when Jesus healed and even brought a number of dead people back to life. That is what was happening when, at the end of his public ministry, God raised him up again after his gruesome death. God not only brought him back to life but raised him into a new quality of life over which death no longer has any power. When Jesus healed, it became clear that in him God's healing and liberating power was present.

The reign of God is not only present when Jesus heals and shows his power over the forces of decay and death. It is also present when Jesus brings people back into fellowship with God, when he restores that primary relationship for which God had created them in the first place. This again is something about which Jesus did not just talk, but which became a reality through his life. One of the most scandalous aspects of Jesus' public activity was that he related to everyone and invited all sorts of people into the circle of his friends and closest followers. As in every society, Jewish society had its outcasts. People with leprosy or degenerative skin diseases were feared because of the infectious nature of their disease and because they were considered ritually 'unclean' – meaning that they could not be fully part of the people of God. Tax-collectors who worked for the occupying power of the Roman Empire were loathed because they were in regular contact with the pagan Romans and because they grew rich on the backs of their own people. Prostitutes were looked down upon because they lived an openly sinful life. These people were shunned by those who considered themselves the elect people of God; they could not be in contact with these outcasts whom they felt were unfit to be part of God's people.

Yet Jesus welcomed these outcasts into his circle; more specifically, he welcomed them to the meals he had with his friends and followers. In most cultures sharing a meal is a sign of intimacy, of sharing lives together. In the Jewish context in which Jesus worked, it had an even deeper meaning. The image of a meal was commonly used to talk about the future of Israel, about the new situation that would be established when God came to save and restore his people: this would be celebrated in festive meals in which the whole people of God would join and be God's guest. When Jesus invited these outcasts into meal-fellowship with him, he was effectively inviting them back into the community of the people of God. He restored them as part of his people. And in searching them out, he represented God looking for the lost in order to bring them back into fellowship with himself.

Who is this Jesus?

Jesus' being and life were therefore so tied up with his message that people around him had a hard time trying to make sense of him and figure out what his relationship with God was. He didn't fit into any of the categories they had at their disposal. The first category that suggested itself was that of a rabbi, a Jewish teacher. Because teaching was one of his core activities, people often addressed him as 'Rabbi'. Yet he was very different from the rabbis with whom they were acquainted. Ordinary rabbis always referred to the teaching of their predecessors and to the words of Moses and the prophets. Even the prophets themselves did not speak on their own behalf and on their own authority, but always introduced their message with a phrase like: 'This is what the Lord God says...' Jesus, though, spoke with direct authority. He placed his own words alongside those of Moses as someone who had the authority to go beyond Moses.

Christians believe that Jesus' authority became even more apparent when he forgave the sins of people he met. The Jews around him knew that only God could forgive sins and that in announcing forgiveness Jesus was implicitly placing himself on the same level as God. Also, rather than calling people to believe God and obey him, he called them to have faith in him and to follow him. He even said that the attitudes people had towards him would be decisive on the day of judgment at the end of history, when God judged their lives. Furthermore, Jesus showed divine authority over the forces of nature when he ordered the winds of a storm to die down and when he ordered evil spirits to leave those whom they had possessed. Jesus gave the gifts only God could give: not just forgiveness, but also new life out of death, eternal life; he gave God's Holy Spirit. He even claimed that when people saw him, they saw God the Father, the Creator of the universe himself.

His opponents took this as blasphemy, and his followers might have equally done so had God himself not confirmed the claims and work of Jesus by raising him from the dead after his gruesome execution on a Roman cross. This was all the more remarkable in that Jesus did not go around shouting from the rooftops: 'Look at me, see how important I am!' He just went about doing what God called him to do, and as he did so, his followers gradually realized that this was not a mere rabbi, or even a prophet. He was the Son of God; he was God himself who had come to live among them.

Fully God and fully human

It is hard to make sense of all this. The difficulty becomes apparent in the way Christians struggle to find appropriate language to say who Jesus was. One moment they call him the 'Son of God', and the next they call him 'God himself living among humankind'. Just as for the Jews at the time, it is hard for people in other cultures and contexts to find appropriate categories to describe this Jesus. The generations of Christians who immediately followed him discovered that this reality stretched all their available ideas and that they needed to develop a whole new vocabulary to do justice to and make sense of this reality.

The discussion about who Jesus Christ was occupied the attention of the finest minds in the Christian communities in the first centuries of the Christian church. The discussion was so complex because what people had heard and read about Jesus and what he meant for them could lead to contradictory conclusions. On the one hand there were indications that Jesus was a human being like all others, yet with a special vocation. One Jewish Christian group called the Ebionites understood him to be essentially that. On the other hand the indications that Jesus was divine were so strong that there were also 'docetist' interpretations of what he was. Docetists believed that Jesus was essentially divine and that his humanness was only a matter of appearance, worn like a garment or mask, which didn't make any essential difference to his divine being.

Most Christian thinkers believed, however, that in order to understand Jesus, one needs to talk about him in both human and divine terms, and that the major question is how these two aspects of him are interrelated. In a number of the so-called 'ecumenical councils' of the church, the issues were settled. These councils were assemblies in which representatives of the churches from all over the regions where Christianity had spread, mainly around the Mediterranean, were present to discuss issues that concerned them all.

In the first ecumenical council, in Nicaea (in today's Turkey) in the year 325, the representatives of the church produced a formula describing Jesus as 'consubstantial' or 'of one nature' with the Father. Their statement that Jesus Christ was fully divine was primarily directed against the influential ideas of a priest called Arius, who said that Jesus was not fully divine, but rather some sort of intermediate being between God and humankind. He wasn't fully God, but God's first and most important creation, and as such much higher than humankind. The gathering of the church in Nicaea rejected this, for they believed that Jesus could never be a half-god. They had inherited the Jewish understanding of God as Creator, and of the world as his creation, with an absolute distinction between the two: there cannot be a halfway house between Creator and creation. They also considered that if Jesus was not truly and fully God, he could not represent God among us, truly reveal God to us, or act as God for our salvation, all things that the Christian Scriptures claimed Jesus did.

In the fourth ecumenical council in the year 451 in Chalcedon (again in Turkey) they went into more depth and discussed the question of how the divine aspect and the human aspect in Jesus Christ were related. One of the positions discussed and rejected at the time was so-called 'Apollinarianism'. According to Apollinarius, Jesus Christ had a human body and a divine soul. This may in fact be what many people both in and outside the church believe the Christian position to be: that Jesus Christ is some hybrid being, partly human, partly divine. The church leaders present at Chalcedon, however, rejected this position as unable to do justice to how God was present in Jesus of Nazareth. If God truly became a human being, he took up human nature in its entirety, body as well as soul. How could God have saved human nature if he had not done so? It is not just the human body that needs saving, but also the human soul. It is human nature in its entirety that is enslaved to sin, that is orientated away from God and is not living in harmony with the world around it as it should be.

That is why the assembly present at Chalcedon concluded that Christians should think of Jesus Christ as fully human and fully divine at the same time, the two sides of his existence being closely united in one personal existence, yet without being changed or becoming less than divine and human. It is possible to argue that such enigmatic formulations do not say very much. It would be more truthful to the original intentions of the people present at Chalcedon to say that these paradoxical expressions are precisely what is needed to do justice to the enigmatic person of Jesus of Nazareth.

In a certain sense the Chalcedonic definition does indeed not say very much: it does not explain precisely how the divine and the human are united in the one person of Jesus of Nazareth. Perhaps it is silent about this in order to respect the mystery of this unique person. It may also be the case that it just indicates the boundaries within which Christians can think about Jesus of Nazareth. It can be seen as an invitation to come up with images and concepts that would help us understand better who this Jesus is, as long as the boundaries are respected: the Scriptures show that he is fully divine; in him God himself is present, reveals himself to us and acts for our salvation. At the same time, the Scriptures show that he is fully human: in Jesus God shared human life with all its joy and suffering and took it into himself in order to save it from slavery to sin and death.

Some critics would claim that the idea of Jesus Christ as both human and divine is not just an enigma; it is simply self-contradictory, rather like saying that a certain shape is a square circle, a shape that cannot exist, and therefore a statement that is meaningless. Assuming that there is a God, it is simply not possible for a God to become a human being. For Christians, this is not so great a problem as it might seem. They would consider it presumptuous to tell God what he can and cannot do. It would presuppose an intimate knowledge of God, and how could that be obtained? How can people who say they have no special knowledge of God claim to know what God can and cannot do? If God himself chose to become 'incarnate' or 'to take on human nature' in Jesus Christ, then why should he not be able to do so? They would also want to stress that 'being God' and 'being human' are not mutually exclusive concepts, as 'being a square' and 'being a circle' are. God himself created human beings modelled on himself or 'in his image' (as we saw in chapter 4), knowing that one day he would want to become a human being himself. It is also important to recall an earlier explanation which says that Christians do not believe that at the time of Jesus of Nazareth God was as it were enclosed in this one human being. Christians believe that God exists as a tri-unity of three persons (chapter 2). As God's Son, God was united with humanity, but as Father, God continued to uphold the universe, and as Spirit, God continued to be intimately present in his entire creation.

The elusive presence of the reign of God

Given that Jesus Christ was fully God and fully human his identity could easily be misunderstood. Because God became fully human, Jesus of Nazareth could be taken for an ordinary human being like anyone else. This parallels the way Christians understand the general pattern of God's presence in the world. God reveals himself in the history of Israel, which on a certain level is a people like any other. God speaks in the Bible, which is not only the Word or message of God, but also a collection of human texts written in different places and at different times in history. That is why the Bible can be studied like any other collection of ancient human documents.

Christians believe that in leaving it at that, however, you would miss the point. It would be like making an effort to understand a letter by doing a chemical analysis of the ink and paper, while missing the message that had been written. The chemical analysis may well be accurate and irrefutable, but it would miss the point of what the letter was about: the chemical components have been used to communicate a message of a different order. This is why, in a certain sense, as the twentieth-century Swiss theologian Karl Barth underlined, God hides himself, even when he reveals himself. Because he reveals himself in history, in a human being and in a human book, his presence can easily be overlooked. Even when present, God always remains elusive.

This does not mean that denying God's presence is an equally sensible interpretation. The chemical analysis of the paper and ink of the letter may be valid, but that does not mean that those who read a message in the writing on the paper are simply projecting ideas from their own imagination. Rather, they encounter a structured message with its own integrity which is able to teach them something new and is even able to challenge what they have thought and imagined so far. Furthermore, the patterns of the signs on the paper remain an enigma that the chemical analysis does not even begin to penetrate. Christians believe that the words of Scripture and the person of Jesus of Nazareth present a message that, far from being a product of their own imagination, impose themselves on them. They remain a mystery that defies reduction to simple human and historic categories.

The person of Jesus of Nazareth does not fit the category of a simple human being. As the Oxford writer C. S. Lewis argued, we cannot think of him as simply a wise man, a religious genius. His teaching about who God is and how we should live, and his relationships with the many people he met, revealed a profound wisdom recognized by Christians and non-Christians alike. Yet in his actions he implicitly claimed to be one with God. His audience rightly saw that if this were not true, such a claim made him a blasphemer. Was it possible for such a person to be regarded as a wise man with profound religious insight? How could a mere human being consider himself equal with God? So was he a blasphemer or was he simply deluded? Christians would say that the deep wisdom of his teaching and the integrity of his life make this hard to swallow. What is more, they believe that God raised him from the dead after he died on the cross and that God thereby confirmed Jesus' far-reaching claims about himself.

There is another dimension to the elusive nature of God's presence in Jesus of Nazareth. It was not just that God was present in human form. More than that, he was present in the form of a weak and fragile human being, who ended his life being abominably executed on a Roman cross. This paradox is aptly captured by the apostle Paul, who wrote that in Jesus Christ the power of God is revealed in weakness, and the wisdom of God looks at first like utter foolishness (1 Corinthians 1:22–25). Jesus showed remarkable power in healing the sick and liberating those bound by demonic forces. Yet he did not use this power in order to make his own life comfortable or to save himself from death. His acceptance of suffering seemed to reveal his weakness, and his willingness to die on a cross seemed absurd. Following Paul, Christians believe that in this weakness and apparent foolishness, God's power was mysteriously present. Rather than fleeing from human suffering, God took human suffering into himself and in the process saved humanity from it. In this way God gave humankind hope in the midst of suffering by giving them hope of a final victory over suffering and death. This was already visible in the resurrection of Christ, in which he conquered death on the third day after he died on the cross.

This leads us to a consideration of the cross of Christ, which Christians believe to be the central event in the life of Christ and in God's work for the salvation of humanity.

What happened on the cross?

Execution

One of the most startling features of the Christian faith is that it has a violent death at the heart of its understanding of God's relationship with humanity, and a cross as its central symbol. This central place, accorded to not just any death, but to the death of Jesus Christ, reflects the structure of the Christian

Scriptures itself. Christians read the Old Testament, the first part of the Christian Scriptures, as leading up to the story of Jesus Christ. In the New Testament, the second part of the Christian Scriptures, the story of Jesus Christ is told four times in the Gospels of Matthew, Mark, Luke and John. These Gospels give four different accounts of the life of Christ, showing that his life had such a multi-layered significance that its meaning cannot be exhausted in a single account. Yet, whatever their differences, all four stories give extended attention to the death of Christ, so much so that someone has called them 'accounts of the death of Christ with prolonged introductions'. The letters of Paul and a couple of other apostles, which form most of the rest of the New Testament, give relatively little attention to the life of Christ but go to great lengths to explain the meaning of the death and resurrection of Christ for the Christian life.

Jesus died on a cross, a method of execution the Romans considered too gruesome for Roman citizens themselves, but which they used to quench all thoughts of rebellion in their large slave population and in the peoples they subjected. Being crucified meant a slow and protracted death. The victims were either fastened or nailed to a crossbeam that was tied to a pole. If they were nailed to the cross, as Jesus was, nails were driven through their wrists and ankles. Hanging on the cross, the victim could not breathe unless he pulled and pushed himself up by the nails holding his wrists and ankles. When he could no longer stand the pain, he would let himself down, till he had to gasp for breath and pull himself up whatever the pain. The process could take anything from couple of hours to a couple of days, until death came either through sheer exhaustion or through blood-poisoning caused by the nails.

All this time, the victim would hang in utter shame, almost or entirely naked, rejected and cursed. What this shame adds to the agony is probably hard to understand for modern Westerners who live in a society where shame and honour are no longer considered very important. Other societies value honour much more, as seen by the fact that in those societies, people will often endure death, even a gruesome death, in order to avoid public shame for themselves or their families. Utter humiliation can be perceived as worse than death.

A truly nauseating image. Yet Christians believe that even this was not the deepest suffering Jesus Christ experienced on the cross. At the time, Jesus' death was far from unique, and his suffering took hours rather than days. The depth of his suffering is shown by the agony Jesus went through in the days leading up to his crucifixion, when he contemplated what he would have to endure. On the evening before his arrest and execution, he prayed for hours in the Garden of Gethsemane, an olive orchard near Jerusalem where he often withdrew when he needed quiet. There he prayed and pleaded with his God the Father, asking whether he could be spared what he called 'this cup' of suffering (Matthew 26:39). This contrasts with many who have faced death with equilibrium and courage, such as Socrates, who quietly drank the cup of poison his executioners had prepared for him. Christians believe that Jesus' agony was not due to a lack of courage. That would be entirely uncharacteristic for him. It was rather a consequence of the fact that what he was due to suffer was more than a physical death. When he referred to 'this cup', he used a biblical image for the anger of God against sin. On the cross, Jesus had to experience the anger of God against sin in order to save humankind from sin and death. In the olive orchard, Jesus finally came to the conclusion that this terrible death could not be avoided. He accepted it willingly, even while he still had the opportunity to escape.

In the Bible and in Christian tradition, different images have been used and different theories have been elaborated in order to understand the importance of the death of Christ. Christ's death has been explained in terms of God's judgment over sin, as a victory over death and the forces of evil, as the supreme revelation of God's love, as Jesus offering himself as a sacrifice to reconcile the world with God, as liberation from the bondage of sin, and as the event through which healing is brought to a hurting world. This plethora of images reflects the many facets of this crucial event, and many Christian thinkers have found that, as in the Bible itself, they need more than one image to explain the richness of what was happening when Christ died on the cross. In what follows we will briefly consider four of the central images used to explain what happened on the cross and in the resurrection of Jesus.

Sacrifice

This first image is one to which most contemporary Westerners relate with difficulty, but which is derived from a common feature of life in the world of the Bible, and is still common in many non-Western societies. In the time of Jesus, the religious life of the Jewish people centred on the Temple in Jerusalem, with its sacrificial system. Every day animals were ritually slaughtered. These sacrifices had a number of functions, one of which was to deal with the sins of the people. The Jews were deeply conscious of the holiness of God, of the fact that God was entirely just and different from this corrupted world. He could not relate to this world unless something was done about the sin and filth of this world. Animals sacrificed for sin underlined this need. It also showed that God himself had in fact done something about sin by providing animals that could be offered to God in exchange for the lives of sinners, who, because of their sin, deserved death themselves.

Jesus indicated that his death should be understood as a

sacrifice for sin. On the night before he died, he had a special meal with his disciples. It had a deeply symbolic meaning which became the basis of the Christian practice of the celebration of the Eucharist or Holy Communion. During this meal Christians share bread and wine. During this first Eucharist, before he died, Jesus referred to the cup of wine as his 'blood' or 'the new covenant in my blood' (Luke 22:20). This was a reference to the earlier covenant God had concluded with Israel under Moses and which had been sealed by the blood of a sacrifice being sprinkled over the people. Jesus indicates that his death is like a sacrifice that seals the new covenant, a new relationship between God and humanity made possible by his death.

Judgment and acquittal

In the Christian tradition, Jesus' death as sacrifice is also closely related to the image of his death freeing us from the judgment of God. This should be understood against the background of the biblical belief that God as the Creator and Lawgiver of the world is also the highest Judge. Because God has given his laws in order to tell human beings how they should live, they are accountable to God for how they conduct their lives. When people do not live according to the will of God, not only do they miss the destination for which they were created, but their lives are also an affront to the God who created them. These ideas come together in the notion of a judgment at the end of history, in which all human beings will have to appear before God and be held accountable for all they have done with their lives.

Christians are deeply conscious that humankind, as a whole – and including Christians, does not live up to the standards God has set for them and that they have therefore forfeited their right to life. Their lives are rightfully condemned by the heavenly Judge. Yet they believe that Jesus' death frees them from this judgment. This idea was elaborately developed by Anselm, an eleventh-century archbishop of Canterbury. It was, however, not a new idea. He developed deeply biblical ideas, not just that about God as a judge, but also about the death of Christ, which was understood against the background of the Old Testament picture of the 'servant of God' who was 'pierced for our transgressions' (Isaiah 53:5).

Anselm understood this to mean that Jesus' willingly dying on the cross gave God the honour sinful humankind had failed to give him. In the time of the Protestant Reformation in the sixteenth century, this idea was developed further when Christ was primarily seen as substituting for humanity in undergoing the punishment humankind deserved. This understanding of the work of Christ became known as the idea of 'penal substitution': on the cross Christ substituted himself for humanity in bearing the judgment of God and the due penalty of sin. This idea is sometimes ridiculed as presupposing a vengeful God who needed to vent his wrath on an innocent victim before he could show mercy. Although it is true that some more poetic expressions of this idea can go in this direction, the proper understanding has always been that God was not punishing an innocent third party instead of humankind, but rather that he carries the consequences of sin himself in becoming human and dying on a cross. The cross of Christ is about God himself bearing away the consequences of human disobedience to him.

Reconciliation

The idea of Christ undergoing the judgment of God or 'the cup of God's wrath' points to an essential aspect of what happened on the cross, yet when taken on its own it risks becoming a truncated understanding of the cross. It might suggest that what happened was merely a legal transaction that could have little consequences for the lives Christians live and of which they will reap the benefits only in the final judgment at the end of history when they will be acquitted of their sin and admitted to heaven. We need to remember, however, that the idea of acquittal of guilt has its place in a larger framework in which humankind is understood to be created in order to live in a special relationship with God as a child lives with his father (see chapter 4). The cross is not about a mere legal transaction, but about reconciliation, about the restoration of a broken relationship.

The apostle Paul says: 'while we were God's enemies, we were reconciled to him through the death of his Son' (Romans 5:10). We saw that this reconciling activity was already taking place during the life of Jesus Christ, when he invited sinners and outcasts to share meals with him and therefore to come back to God and join his fellowship. Paul indicates that this reconciling work of Jesus during his life culminated in his death on the cross. Somehow this death was necessary in order to bring humankind back to God, in order to turn human beings from enemies of God into friends of God. Left to themselves, human beings just go on living as if God does not exist. Or if they do accept the existence of some sort of a God, they try to picture him in ways designed to keep him at bay or that make it possible to manipulate him so that he serves petty human interests.

Christians understand that that is what idolatry is about: making God into an idol, possibly an image that you can carry around. You can carry it at the head of your army in order to give you victory; you can place its temple in your capital city to make your nation great; or you can nail it over the door of your business in order to make you rich. These may be relatively crude forms of idolatry, but Christians believe that modern people, religious or not, have their own more or less sophisticated ways to keep God at bay or to use him for their own interests. They believe that modern people have their own ways of living their lives estranged from God or even in enmity with God. They believe that modern people are equally in need of reconciliation with God, of restoring this relationship which should be central to their lives.

Christians believe that this is what happened when Jesus died on the cross. God did not wait for humanity to change and turn back to him. He knows that left to themselves they would never do this. That is why he actively searches to restore this relationship himself. That is why he sent his Son into the world. That is why he did not hit back when humankind rejected this Jesus rather than accepted his message. God kept loving them, even when it meant Jesus dying on the cross, utterly rejected by the people of the time. Yet, in doing so, he showed that his love was stronger than the enmity of humankind, and in the process humankind was changed. The love of God, which became most visible in the cross of Jesus Christ, began to change people from the inside out, and to turn them from enemies of God into his friends.

Victory

A final image used to explain what happened on the cross is the image of victory, a notion that belongs originally to the world of battles and wars. In the last chapter, we saw that for Christians, the ideas of sin and evil are not exhausted when we describe them in terms of the wrong and destructive choices people make in life. Sin is also a power that enslaves. How people live is largely determined by their past experiences, by the life they have lived until now and by the societies in which they live. Sometimes they find themselves wanting to live entirely different lives, following different priorities, with different attitudes to God and the people around them. Yet reality is hard, and it is difficult to change ingrained attitudes and gut reactions. People are enslaved by the sinful patterns of their lives and societies.

The writers of the Bible do not just understand this as enslavement in terms of psychological chains to past experiences, ingrained habits and social pressures that steer people's lives. They talk about spiritual, demonic powers that oppress humankind. Some modern Christians would reinterpret this language as an ancient, mythological way of speaking about the common psychological and social realities to which we just referred. Other Christians believe that this language about demonic powers expresses something essential about how evil works. The unmitigated evils of the twentieth century, of Stalinism and the Holocaust, of Pol Pot in Cambodia and of the atrocities of colonial exploitation at its worst have helped to convince them that there is something superhuman about the power of evil. Evil is not only the result of human behaviour, but holds humanity in its grip.

Many non-Western Christians have a worldview in which the universe is more overtly filled with all sorts of spiritual powers between heaven and earth. They therefore relate naturally to these biblical images of Satan and evil spirits and of the angels who serve God and come to the aid of humankind. The biblical idea that the cross of Christ is a victory over the spiritual powers of evil that hold humankind in its grip is therefore hugely popular in churches in Africa, Latin America and Asia, and in the many churches of ethnic minorities in Europe and North America.

The New Testament tells stories about how Jesus during his life on earth confronted Satan and evil spirits head on. He drove them out and liberated the so-called possessed people they held in their grip. The New Testament explains the cross as the decisive victory over these forces. These powers of darkness, evil and death thought they had overpowered their most formidable opponent by having him nailed to the cross. Yet after three days Jesus came back to life, rose from the dead and thereby showed himself to be stronger than these powers of evil. Christians therefore believe that the strongest forces that hold humankind enslaved – Satan, sin and death – have been conquered by Christ. Even death has no hold over them, because they believe that just as God raised Jesus Christ to a new and incorruptible life, so God will also raise them at the end of time to live life in its fullness.

For Christians, this spiritual battle and victory are closely related to their day-to-day lives. It is an answer to the power of their sinful attitudes and habits and to the way the society in which they live hugely limits their freedom to live fulfilling lives. The cosmic victory on the cross and the daily battle of Christians are linked through the gift of the Holy Spirit. As we saw, the Holy Spirit is the third person of the three-in-one God and has therefore always existed. Yet after the resurrection of Christ, the Spirit of God became active in the world in an entirely new way. Fifty days after Jesus Christ rose from the dead, the Spirit of God was given to humankind and especially to the Christian community. From now on, the followers experienced the presence of God much more intimately and strongly. The power of the living Christ who had conquered sin and death was present in their life. This renewed their lives and gave them the inner power to live differently from their past and from the world around them. As followers of Christ, they became agents of the kingdom of God. In them, the authority and rule of God over the world became visible in a new way. What, or rather who, this Spirit is, and what Christians believe about his presence in the world, will occupy our attention in the next chapter.

In this chapter, we have explored some aspects of what Christians believe about Jesus Christ. We saw that this meaning is incredibly rich and cannot be explained with the help of just a single image. He is the Conqueror over the powers of evil and death, the deepest and most radical expression of the love of God who reconciles us with him, the Judge of the universe who is judged in our place, the sacrifice for our sins, the Son of God, who reveals the Father to humankind, and the inaugurator of the reign of God.

This list is far from exhaustive, and its length is not only due to the fact that this crucial event in the heart of history has so many meanings and has changed the course of history so radically. It is also related to the fact that this one person has followers all over the world. While joining the worldwide Christian community, these followers also retain much of their cultural distinctiveness, as we saw in the introduction to this book. This is why some relate to him first and foremost as the Conqueror of death, others as the Healer of the deepest wounds of their lives, and others again as their truest soulmate. This is a sign of what we noted in the introduction: that Jesus is at home in many different worlds. Christians believe, however, that he is not present in all these worlds in order to leave them as they are, but to transform them radically as people become gradually aware of new sides of this Jesus and of the message of his kingdom and as they grow in their lives with him.

6. The Spirit of God and the Christian Community

The gift of the Spirit of God

Good Friday, Easter, Ascension, Pentecost

Their precise dates may differ, but every spring all the main Christian traditions celebrate four closely related events. On a Friday called Good Friday, they commemorate the death of Christ on the cross in Palestine around the year 30 AD. On the following Sunday, they celebrate Easter, the most important of all Christians feasts, when they remember how Jesus Christ came back to life on the third day. It is a central element of the Christian faith that this was a bodily resurrection: the same person who was buried came back to life, not in some ghostly disembodied form but in his own recognizable body. Though it still was a bodily existence, it had undergone radical change. It was imbued with the life of God and was therefore no longer subject to death and decay. We will come back to this astonishing feature in the last chapter when we consider what Christians believe about the end of time.

Though Jesus Christ came back to life, Christians do not believe that you can go somewhere specific, say to Jerusalem, and meet him in person. This has to do with the third event, called 'Ascension', celebrated on a Thursday forty days after Easter. According to the Gospel of Luke, Jesus Christ met his followers regularly in the forty days after his resurrection. After that he went back to heaven. This going to 'heaven' should not be understood in a spatial sense, as if Jesus Christ made a space journey starting from some place near Jerusalem and ending somewhere in the universe where heaven could be located. In the Christian Scriptures, heaven is the place were God lives and where nothing opposes God's reign. It may be that many early Christians imagined it as a place somewhere above the earth, but it need not be imagined in that way in the universe as modern science understands it, a universe that expands for billions of light-years in all directions. Some contemporary Christian scientists therefore think of heaven as a space that extends in a number of dimensions beyond the three or four dimensions in which we live. Jesus' ascension to heaven would then mean that he moved from a limited existence within this created universe into the space or sphere of God, which exists in dimensions different from those of the ordinary universe. There may be indications of this in the Bible stories that talk about the risen Jesus as truly having a body, yet not being bound by the same spatial limitations as ordinary human beings. He could, for example, suddenly appear and disappear.

However Christians picture this ascension to heaven, its central meaning is that Jesus has gone back to the sphere of God the Father. Although Christians do sometimes long to meet Jesus just as his contemporaries could meet him, they believe that Jesus' departure was no loss. Jesus himself said that he would need to leave so that the Spirit of God could come (John 16:7). The Spirit of God is a different presence of God among humankind, more intimate even than his personal presence in Jesus Christ, and no longer confined to one place as was the human presence of God in Christ.

The way God is increasingly present among humankind is evident in the use of the image of 'temple' in the Bible. The idea of a temple, a sacred building where people would go to meet their god, was well known in antiquity. In the same way the people of Israel had its Temple in Jerusalem, where God had promised to be present among them. In the New Testament, however, Jesus himself is called the temple of God (John 2:18–21). God's presence was now concentrated in this one person. God had never been this close. In the following stage, towards the end of the Bible, Christians themselves are called the temple of God, because the Spirit of God lives in them (1 Corinthians 6:19). God's presence is no longer focused in a building or person; rather, he lives in all who open up their lives to him. The God who showed his face and heart most truly and clearly in Jesus Christ is now making this love universally available. The Spirit of God living in them relates Christians today directly to Jesus Christ, who lives now with God the Father. That is why Christians say not only that the Spirit of God lives in them, but also that Jesus lives in them.

It is at the feast of Pentecost, ten days after Ascension Day and fifty days after Easter Sunday, that Christians celebrate this gift of the Spirit, this new and renewing presence of God. They commemorate the first Pentecost, when, after a period of waiting following the ascension of Jesus, his first band of followers received the gift of the Spirit of God.

It is important to note that all these Christian feasts celebrate historical events, though not ordinary historical events. God is at work here in an extraordinary way, yet he works in history through these events that changed the course of history. These Christian feasts aren't celebrations of the cycles of nature that recur every year. Nor are they celebrations of mythical legends that tell of events that did not happen historically, but that convey eternal truths about human existence. These Christian festivals celebrate events that happened in history at a specific time and place and that, according to Christian belief, for ever changed the world.

The Spirit of God

The Spirit is often named 'the Spirit of God' or 'the Holy Spirit'. Both expressions point to the divine nature of the Spirit. When people refer to the 'spiritual side' of life, they often mean some spiritual dimension of all reality or more generally to personal or impersonal spiritual forces they believe exist in the universe. Christians share the belief that there is a spiritual depth to human existence, and that as a spiritual being every human has a need for God. Most Christians also believe that there are other spiritual beings in the universe, be they angels or demons. Yet these spirits are created by God and are not divine. The Holy Spirit is different in that he is divine. He is part of the inner life of the trinitarian God himself. As we saw before, Christians understand God to exist as a tri-unity, as Father, Son and Spirit, all equally God, even one God, but existing as a relationship of three persons (chapter 2). The fact that this Spirit is not just any spirit, but the Spirit of God himself, is directly tied to a number of important ideas: he is, in the language of ancient Christian summaries of faith, the 'Lord, the giver of life'. He is the presence of God himself among his people, the personalized love and life of God poured out into human lives.

If this Spirit is God himself, human beings are called to obey him as Master of their lives. So many human religious practices are about mastering spiritual forces. This is true of the many religions sometimes called 'animistic'. People in these traditional religions, in Africa or elsewhere, will go to witchdoctors or fetishists in search of healing, success in business or politics, or the harm of their enemies. The better these religious specialists are in mastering these spiritual powers, the more successful they are felt to be. Some Western forms of spiritualism and occult practices are not very different. For people with such backgrounds there is a risk that they might approach the Holy Spirit in the same way: as a spiritual force to be mastered to their advantage, yet more powerful than all other spirits. That is what people then expect from Christian healers and miracle-workers. However, if the Spirit of God is holy and divine, it also means that he is Lord. Living a life imbued by the power of the Spirit is, for Christians, not about mastering the Spirit, but about letting their lives be directed by the Spirit, letting him be Lord over their lives. That will then lead to a life that in various ways will look like the life of Jesus Christ himself, in whom the power of the Spirit was most visible. What that means will become clearer in the next chapter, which will concentrate on the Christian life.

This Spirit is also called the 'giver of life'. That alone links this Spirit directly to God, for only God can give life. God gave the universe and humankind existence and life by creating it. The Spirit of God was also present and active in this first act of creation, yet Christians believe that the Spirit of God has a particular role in what they call 're-creation', the renewal of creation. As we saw, Christians believe this created universe to be originally good, yet suffering the destructive consequences of sin and death. It is the Spirit of God who has a crucial role in renewing this creation, in giving it new life. This new life became a reality with the resurrection of Jesus Christ from death. It is the vocation of the Holy Spirit to share this new life of Christ with humankind and with the entire universe. Christians believe that no spiritual force other than the Holy Spirit can give this new life, and that he can do so precisely because he is the Spirit of the Creator God.

The Spirit of Jesus

The Holy Spirit is not only linked to the God of Creation, but also to Jesus. The Holy Spirit is the Spirit who empowered and guided Jesus of Nazareth and who in turn was given by the risen Jesus Christ to his followers. The fact that this Spirit is the eternal Spirit of God, present at creation, yet given in a new way by Jesus at Pentecost, shows that Christians distinguish different phases in the activity of the Spirit. The Holy Spirit has always been there as a sustaining and life-giving presence of God within the universe. In the history of the people of Israel, the Spirit also had a role in inspiring prophets when they gave the message of God to his people, and in guiding liberators, kings and priests as they gave direction to the people of God. During the earthly life of Jesus of Nazareth, the presence and activity of the Holy Spirit were particularly focused in his life, in how the liberating presence of God became a visible reality in him.

Christians can therefore recognize the life-sustaining presence of the Spirit everywhere in the universe and in society. They believe, however, that God has given his Spirit in a special way to the followers of Jesus, to those who have embraced Jesus and his gifts, including this most marvellous gift of the Spirit. This does not mean that Christians want to keep this gift to themselves. Rather they consider themselves as called to share this life-giving Spirit of Jesus with everyone they encounter.

The gifts of the Spirit

When we take this a step further and ask where Christians see the Spirit of God particularly at work, we discover that different Christian traditions tend to give different answers. Let us consider some of the main traditions, beginning with the oldest ones. We need to note at the outset that these different understandings of the Spirit's work are not necessarily at odds with each other. In each tradition, you will find Christians who appreciate elements from the other traditions and see them as valuable enrichments of their own.

The Spirit of deification and new creation

The Eastern Orthodox traditions place a particular emphasis on the Spirit as the renewing presence of God within creation. As we indicated earlier, this renewal is understood in terms of 'deification' or 'becoming divine'. Even though human beings can never become divine themselves, they were created in order that they might participate in the divine life.

This participation was first of all a reality in the life of Jesus, who was himself the God-man in a unique way: he was himself by nature both human and divine. Yet in a different sense, through Jesus Christ and his Spirit, all those who follow Christ can also participate in the divine life when the Spirit lives in them and when they become the temple of God. This process begins in the lives of Christians when the Spirit enters their lives. It will be complete when, after their death, they will be brought into the presence of God and become part of the heavenly worshipping community of those who praise God and enjoy his presence. It will be perfect at the end of history when God will be 'all in all', when his Spirit will have penetrated, renewed and revived the entire universe.

For Orthodox Christians, the weekly celebration in their church meetings is the moment when they have a first taste of what this deification will be. Weekly church reunions are not just meetings of a number of people who share the same religious interests. Orthodox Christians believe that the liturgy of these services – the ceremonial acts and language used in these meetings – mirrors the heavenly liturgy in which the angels and deceased believers worship God. When they gather in church they join in this heavenly liturgy. This is a piece of heaven on earth. They are not just taken up into heaven, they are taken up into the life of God himself, because they are not just praying by themselves: the Holy Spirit living in them is praying and worshipping through them, and so they are taken up into the love-life of the triune God himself.

The Spirit of the Word of God and regeneration

In the Protestant tradition which started with the European Reformation of the sixteenth century, the Spirit is seen to be particularly at work through the preaching of the gospel message. This is considered the primary manner through which God leads the church and renews and changes people today. The Spirit of God is therefore closely related to the Bible as the Word of God. When the Bible is read and explained, people are not just listening to human words. Through these words God himself is speaking to them, because these words are believed to be inspired by God the Holy Spirit himself.

This also helps us understand the important place of the sermon in Protestant church services. The sermon is the central element of these meetings, in which the pastor or another leader of the community reads a passage of the Bible and explains what it means today. This is so central to them because Protestants believe that in this way God himself speaks to them. Christians know, of course, that their pastors do not always understand the Bible well and do not always speak the truth, but they do believe that the Holy Spirit wants to use these limited human beings to share the message of God with others. This also explains why Protestant Christians, in particular, have worked so hard to get the Bible translated into as many languages as possible. This is an enormous task, but it is crucial if all are to hear God speak to them in their own language. The same conviction is reflected in the practice of daily Bible reading. Many Christians read the Bible on a daily basis, on their own or with their families or friends. This is how they seek to meet God and find his guidance for their lives.

For Christians, this listening to the Bible is not just about learning new ideas about God. They believe that when the Holy Spirit speaks to them through the Bible, this Word of God has the power to renew them. In chapter 4 we discussed the reality of sin and saw that Christians believe that sin is not just a wrong choice, but a power that enslaves people and alienates them from God. When God speaks to them through the Bible, this alienation is reversed, because God comes close to them where they are. And through these words the Spirit of God works powerfully to change them. This is how the Spirit 'regenerates' people, so that they become 'born again' Christians. From then on, they can begin leading new lives, lives renewed by the Spirit of God.

This regeneration or new birth is considered to be a one-off event. When people call themselves 'born-again' Christians, they want to indicate that they have experienced this renewing power of God in their lives. By using this term, they are of course at the same time making another statement: that they are the type of Christian for whom the notion of 'being born again' is crucial: you cannot be a Christian just by natural birth or tradition. It needs to change your life. Sadly, particularly in North America, being a 'born-again' Christian has become a political label for people who identify with certain political pressure groups, and this can sometimes obscure the deep religious meaning of the idea of 'new birth'.

Although this new birth or regeneration is believed to be a one-off event, the Christian life is believed to be one in which people can grow in their relationship with God. Here again, the Holy Spirit speaking though the Bible is considered to be the renewing power who makes this gradual change possible. When Christians meet in church or in small groups in their homes, they listen to what God has to say to them through the Bible. This is how they invite the Holy Spirit to work in them so that their lives may be changed and become more like the exemplary life of Jesus.

The Spirit of power and healing

One of the most vibrant Christian movements of the twentieth century and the beginning of the twenty-first is the Pentecostal movement, which has grown spectacularly. It started in its current form as recently as the beginning of the last century, but has had a huge impact not only in North America, where it originated, but also in Latin America, Africa and Asia, where it resonates with people's sense of the spiritual dimensions of life. Its growth outside the older Christian church traditions runs parallel with the growth of the so-called 'charismatic movement' in the older churches, which has a similar understanding of the work of the Holy Spirit, and gets its name from the 'charismata' or 'gifts' of the Spirit. At the turn of the millennium, possibly 400,000 people worldwide considered themselves Pentecostal or charismatic Christians.

The Pentecostal movement defines itself in terms of its experience of a new feast of Pentecost, a new experience of the Holy Spirit. They believe that the traditional message of forgiveness of sin through faith in Jesus Christ is not the full gospel message. God wants to give much more: he wants to give his people the fullness of his Spirit through a special 'baptism' in the Spirit. The more common use of the word 'baptism' refers to a defining moment at the beginning of the Christian life. It is a ritual that signifies one's becoming a part of the community of God, either by immersion under water or by the sprinkling of water on new Christians, be they babies, children or adults. Pentecostal Christians believe that just as Christians are baptized with water in water baptism, they should also be 'immersed' by the Spirit in Spirit baptism. The Holy Spirit should fill them with the love, presence and power of God.

It may be that to the outside world, Pentecostal Christians are mostly known for their exuberant church services in which all sorts of strange things are said to be happening, such as miraculous healings, prophetic speech and so-called speaking in tongues. When these Christians speak or sing in tongues, the express themselves with words and sounds that would not ordinarily be known to people around them. This is nowadays mostly seen as a form of praying under the guidance of the Holy Spirit. Some of the deepest human needs, but also some of the highest praise of God, cannot be expressed in ordinary language, and the Holy Spirit helps people to express these in a language they may not understand but that God does. Pentecostal Christians also expect God to speak through so-called 'prophetic words' in which the Holy Spirit guides a member of the Christian community to speak God's message to them, in order to guide them in their lives. Miraculous healings also are given a central place, because this is where the Spirit not only manifests his power, but also shows his deep desire for humankind to live healed and whole lives. This healing is sometimes physical, but Christians believe that the Spirit also does his work of inner healing in dealing with people's inner hurts and scars that they carry with them from their past and that hamper their relationship with God and with the people around them in the present. God wants people to flourish, and the healing power of the Spirit is given to overcome all powers that hinder such flourishing.

This overview of movements which have accentuated different aspects of the work of the Holy Spirit is far from complete. A fuller overview would need to talk about liberation theology which originated among oppressed communities in Latin America and that stresses the work of the Holy Spirit in movements that strive for liberation and fight the unjust structures in this world. It would need to touch on the holiness movements that place a particular stress on the special work of the Spirit in the renewal of the lives of Christians, so that they may live holy lives in which they conquer the destructive influence of sin. A wider overview would also need to discuss the worldwide missionary movement, which emphasizes the role of the Holy Spirit in sending out Christians all over the world in order to tell people from all nations and cultures about Jesus Christ so that they may embrace the good news of the salvation he brings. Given that Christians believe that the Spirit brings the salvation obtained by Christ to bear on all areas of life, it is not surprising that they can stress different aspects of his work. This is why many Christians are open to recognizing that the Spirit works in ways and in areas of life other than those they focus on in their own tradition.

In considering this overview of everything Christians believe the Holy Spirit does in the world, it is important to remember that for Christians the greatest gift of the Spirit is not what he does for humankind. The greatest gift is the Holy Spirit himself. God gives himself to humankind so that they may share in his life and experience his love.

The church as the people of God

The people of God

For Christians, Pentecost is not only the feast of the gift of the Holy Spirit. The first Pentecost is also the day the church came into existence. When Christians talk about the church in this sense, they do not primarily mean buildings called churches or organizations such as the Roman Catholic Church, the Lutheran Church or the Anglican Church. They primarily mean the community of those who believe in Jesus of Nazareth as the Saviour of the world. That this community needs organizational structures and buildings as meeting-places is secondary to this belief that they are united as a community because of what God did for them through Jesus.

In an important sense, the church as the community of believers and as the people of God is much older than Pentecost. Christians would see the people of Israel in the time of the Bible as a precursor of the church. This people was chosen by God to be his people. God had made himself known to them in a special way through Moses and the prophets who spoke God's message to them. They were set apart from the other nations and called to demonstrate what it meant to live as the people of God. Similarly, the band of Jesus' first disciples, who followed him for the couple of years during which he proclaimed the coming kingdom of God, represented the seeds of what would become the church.

Yet Christians believe that the church as we know it now came into existence only at the first Pentecost, when the Holy Spirit was given. The community of believers in Jesus who were gathered that day received the Holy Spirit as the gift of the risen and living Jesus Christ. The Spirit was the power of the new creation, of the new life that had become a reality through the death and resurrection of Jesus. That community assembled in Jerusalem in the early thirties of the first century AD was the beginning of the worldwide church that we know today.

The Christian Scriptures and, following them, Christian thinkers, use many different images to illustrate the nature of the church. The church is compared to 'the flock' of the Good Shepherd, Jesus Christ, who takes care of and leads his followers. It is called 'the bride of Christ', a daring image indicating that the Christian community finds its destiny when it is united with Christ in a loving relationship, as a bride and bridegroom are united in love. It is called 'the temple of God', highlighting that through his Holy Spirit God himself lives in the church. It is described as 'the body of Christ' to show that by his Spirit Christians are closely united in Christ and that through his Spirit-filled church Jesus Christ himself is present in the world. It is also called 'the people of God', the community of people who define themselves not in terms of national identity or social status, but in terms of their relationship with Jesus Christ. They belong to him.

The idea of the church as the people of God may be one of the more accessible images for the church. In order to understand what Christians believe about what the church is, however, we also need the other images. Otherwise the impression might be given that the church is simply a gathering or community of people with similar religious opinions. Christians believe that the church is much more than that. It is a community in which God himself is present and in which the seeds of the new creation are already sown. The church can therefore also be called the 'first-fruits' (James 1:18). This rather archaic word has a deep meaning in traditional agricultural societies. The first-fruits are the beginning of the harvest. They are not just a promise of the harvest, but its beginning. The church as the community of believers is the beginning of the new creation which will be completed when, at the end of history, the entire universe will be redeemed and renewed.

What makes a church a church?

Christians have done significant thinking on what marks out the true church and distinguishes it from those communities that call themselves a Christian church, yet that lack something essential. This question does not just grow from an unhealthy but all-too-human desire to write others off as second-rate Christians. It is a legitimate question, motivated by the desire to be the type of church that God wants his people to be. Christians have given at least four main answers that reflect different understandings of the nature of the Christian community.

A first group regards the church primarily as an institution. This approach particularly characterizes certain Roman Catholic understandings of the church, which stress that the true church needs to be united via its bishops to its institutional head, the pope in Rome. This stress on appropriate institutional links is motivated on the one hand by the belief that the church can guard the unity of its faith only when it is linked to the first generation of followers of Jesus Christ via the succession of bishops and popes. The first disciples, especially those among them with special authority, called apostles, handed down the true teachings concerning Jesus. The bishops and the pope, who have received these teachings and hand them on to the next generation, are thereby able to keep the church to its true faith and protect it against erroneous teaching. Equally important is the belief that only those who are rightly ordained as priests of the church as successors of Jesus and the apostles, truly mediate God's grace and salvation to present-day believers. They do this particularly through the sacraments, such as baptism and the Eucharist, which we will discuss later in this chapter.

A second group of churches emphasizes the faithful preaching of the Bible as the Word of God and the faithful administration of the sacraments as the marks of the true church. This is especially true in the Protestant churches originating in the European Reformation. It corresponds with the belief that the Holy Spirit guides the church primarily through the Bible as pastors explain its teaching and as members of the Christian community read it for themselves.

Pentecostal and charismatic Christians, thirdly, point to the powerful presence of the Holy Spirit as the mark of the true church. According to them, an institutional church can become ossified and dead, as can the explanation of the Word of God if it becomes no more than a lifeless repetition of ancient truths. The Holy Spirit mediates the power and presence of the risen Jesus Christ and thereby guides the church today.

A fourth stream stresses not so much what the church is and does for its members, but what it should do for the world around it. The church does not exist for itself, but for the world. The church should work to make the world a better place and to make it more human, more just. Only in contributing to the building of a just and peaceful world can the church be true to its calling and nature.

As we have seen before, when listing a number of different positions, these understandings of the church are not mutually exclusive. When developed to its extreme, an institutionalized church looks very different from a church where people seek the guidance and presence of the Spirit today. Yet charismatic movements stressing the freedom of the Spirit need some form of structure to help them distinguish between true and false, healthy and unhealthy spiritual experiences. On the other hand, the institutional church needs the presence of the Spirit to keep it alive and powerful, and the preaching of the Word to continually invigorate it with the message of the good news of Jesus Christ. The church is indeed called to proclaim this message, and a Christian community that isolates itself and turns into itself forfeits its calling. Yet a church will have a message for the world and will be able to contribute to the fight for justice and peace only when it has something to share. It needs to be constantly renewed by the presence of Jesus Christ through the Holy Spirit by the preaching of the Scriptures and the celebration of the sacraments. This is why it is so important that the different church traditions do not isolate themselves from one another. It is only when they encounter one another that they can learn from the strength and riches of other Christian communities and will also be able to recognize the weaknesses and limitations of their own understanding of what it means to be the church or the people of God.

The mission of the church

The church and the world

To understand the nature of the church, it is also important to ask what Christians believe about the purpose of the church. Many of our discussions elsewhere in this pocket guide have important implications for the answer to this question. In our discussion of the Christian understanding of humankind as created in the image of God (chapter 4) we discussed the Christian belief that there are three relationships that are essential for the flourishing of humanity. Human beings are meant to flourish in developing right relationships with God, with the community in which they participate and with the non-human creation which they are called to creatively develop and care for. The church as the vanguard of the new creation is the community where people learn how to live out these three relationships in a renewed way. The church reveals a new way to be human, the way it was originally intended to be.

As the people of God and the first-fruits of the new creation, the church does not exist for its own sake. Christians believe that the church exists first of all for the sake of God. They are called to praise and worship God and give him all the honour that is due to him. As we saw in chapter 3, people are invited to praise God more than anything else because he is more worthy and praiseworthy, and because in praising him they enjoy God.

The church also exists for the world around it. It is true that the church often has a tendency to be inward-looking, to be more concerned about its own survival and well-being. Yet Christians do believe that in an important sense the church exists for the sake of the world around it. In the period since the ascension of Jesus and the gift of the Holy Spirit at Pentecost, the church has a particular role in God's rescue plan for the world. When Jesus left the world he called on the disciples to proclaim the good news of salvation all over the earth. That is what has been happening since the church began in Jerusalem and started to spread out all over all the continents, a movement we described in the introduction.

In this process, the Christian faith became the first truly global community, but not in the sense in which capitalism is a global force, overpowering all local economic spheres. As a global community, the church is multicultural, showing that the Christian faith can be expressed in different cultural terminologies and clothing and lived out in different cultural contexts. For Christians, the continuing spread of the church through the centuries and across the world is more than a historical process driven by human ideals and interests. Christians see this as the work of God, who is at work through the church to make Jesus Christ known all over the world so that his salvation may be experienced by all.

The church and its members

In order to be the vanguard of the new world, the church should be not only outward-looking, but also looking after itself and its own members. Christians believe that the church is the place where people can enter into the reality of a new relationship with God and of living as renewed people. Many of the activities of the Christian community offer occasions to experience this new relationship with God and this new community, and to build the church members up so that they grow in their faith and life with God and become more like the people and community God wants them to be.

Being part of a church is not just a Sunday thing for Christians, but their weekly church services are a focal point for their Christian existence. Christians believe that their time should be spent in the service of God and in living out the love and grace of God. Yet for most of them a large chunk of their time is taken up with activities in which God does not get much explicit attention: when they do their housework, go to work or to school. In order to live fully as the people of God, they need specific times when they can concentrate on God, relate to him and reflect on their lives again in the light of his love and grace.

That is why many Christians and Christian families have moments during the day when they take time for prayer and often also to read the Bible. That is also why Christians set apart one day, Sunday, as a special day for God. Christians believe that having such a day of rest from one's ordinary activities is good for everyone. That is why Christians often campaign to make or keep Sunday a special day on which as many business and workplaces as possible are closed. This is how they express that earning money and growing the economy are not the only important things in life, and not even the most important. It is an act of resistance against the moneymakers who reduce human life to how much net profit people can make or to how much they can consume.

For Christians, Sunday serves not just to interrupt economic activities and to provide a day of rest. It also has a more positive meaning as the day in which they take time to refocus their lives on God and find strength to live through him. That is why church meetings or services form a crucial element in the Christian Sunday. The character of such services may vary significantly across Christian denominations, but they generally contain similar elements. When we consider these different elements, we will understand why they are so important for their members.

Church services are times for prayer and worship. In worship, Christians express in songs, music and words their praise of God, acknowledging how great he is, how much he has done for them, and how much they love him. In their prayers they express their deepest desires and needs before God, asking him for help and entrusting themselves to him. In doing so they experience their love for God and their dependency on God much more intensely than they would ordinarily do during the rest of the week, but also refocus and calibrate their lives so that God is at the forefront of their lives during the rest of the week.

Church services are also places where the Scriptures are read and explained. As we saw above, Christians believe that through the Bible God himself speaks to them, giving them a deeper understanding of who they are before God and how they should live.

When Christians meet God in worship and listen to his message, they not only see the greatness of God, but are also confronted with their own weaknesses, sins and failures. They realize that they do not live up to the ideals that God has set before them. In the light of the perfect nature and beauty of God, they discover that their own lives do not measure up. That is why they constantly need to receive God's forgiveness and renewing power. This happens when, in a special prayer in the service, the people confess their sins to God and ask for forgiveness, and this forgiveness is promised to them.

This renewing of the people happens in a special way in the celebration of the sacraments. Sacraments are symbolic acts that play a crucial role in how God shares his love with humanity and gives them his grace. Different church traditions have varied numbers of sacraments, but most churches recognize at least the two most important: baptism and the Eucharist, or Holy Communion.

Baptism is a ritual in which either infants or adults are immersed in water or sprinkled with it. This happens once in a lifetime when someone becomes a member of the church. The water is a sign of the person's purification from all the sins that separate people from God and make them unfit to be members of the people of God. Immersion in water also signifies that the persons are seen as dying to their former existence – going down into the water being compared to burial. Yet, as the person is raised out of the water, they are seen as rising again into a new existence, as a new creation and a member of the people of God. When water is only sprinkled, this symbolism is less clear, but it is seen as pointing to the same reality.

While baptism is a one-off event in the life of Christians, the celebration of Holy Communion or the Eucharist is not. In this sacrament, the members of the church all receive a small piece of bread or a wafer and in many cases also a sip of wine. Like baptism, this is a ritual which Christians believe was begun by Jesus Christ himself. We already explained how on the evening before he died on the cross, Jesus shared bread and wine with his disciples as the sign of the new covenant. When doing so, he said that the bread represented his body and the wine his blood; it pointed to his death, when his body was broken and his blood was shed for them in order to inaugurate this new relationship with God. When Christians today share bread and wine in the Eucharist they therefore remember the death of Jesus Christ for their salvation. They believe that in participating in this ritual meal they in some way have a part in the death and in the new life of the now risen Christ.

The church between ideal and reality

Much of the language used about the church in these pages can sound rather idealistic and therefore unrealistic. How sensible is it to speak about the church as the people of God? How realistic to talk about the church as the place where people can learn to flourish in their relationship with God and with the people around them? The institutional church seems to be all too human. When we notice the power games it sometimes plays and the self-interest and fear that guide many of its decisions it doesn't look very different from other human organizations. The church has not only brought people near to God, but has estranged people from God too, and has been an object of distrust and even hatred. The church is seen as the first-fruits of the new creation, but it often looks rather ancient and more of a conservative force than a radical, innovating and renewing one. For many non-Christians, the church is one of the factors that most puts them off taking Christian belief more seriously. If the church is what these beliefs produce, surely there is something not quite right with the beliefs. Many Christians would disagree, while at the same time believing that the church can and should be very different from what it is.

Thankfully this is not the only side of the coin. In the history of the church, Christian communities have shown incredible courage in denouncing injustice and in demonstrating a deep love in caring for the outcasts of society. Many Christians have also shown how the love of God transformed them, giving them love for people who hated them, courage in very difficult circumstances and hope when everything seemed hopeless. They have kept their faith in God, for their faith was not so much about the quality of the church or about what the church could do for the world as about God himself. Their faith was about what God has done and is still going to do to rescue humanity. Their love is not primarily for the church, but for the God of the church, whose beauty, greatness and love surpass everything else they know.

Yet the tension remains between the reality of what the church is and the ideal of what it is meant to be and believed to be. Christian thinkers have therefore often made a distinction between the visible and the invisible church. The visible church is the failing institution, the ailing community, of people who call themselves Christians. The invisible church is a spiritual reality, the community of true believers who make up only a part of the visible church. It is the church as it exists in the eyes of God, who forgives all its shortcomings and amazingly sees it as the beautiful bride of Christ, whatever its external appearance.

The risk in making this distinction obviously lies in the possibility that Christians might become less concerned about the failings of the visible church as it exists. More importantly, according to Christian belief, this visible Christian community remains the place where God is at work, changing people, and where God's love should be reflected in renewed people who form a loving community as the first-fruits of the new creation. It might be helpful to think about the tension between reality and ideal not only in terms of what is visible and invisible, but also in terms of God's salvation that is already a reality in the world but is not yet complete, and for which Christians are still waiting as something to come at the end of history.

These terms 'already' and 'not yet' are often used to express biblical thinking about God's rescue plan. Through Jesus Christ,

God conquered death when Christ rose from the dead to new life. Christians experience the power of the resurrection and new life, yet they still die and wait for the resurrection of all humankind at the end of history. God's salvation is made real to individuals in the gift of the Spirit who lives in Christians and changes them from the inside out. Yet Christians know that they are in the process of being changed, and are far from the finished product. Because God does not force his love on anyone, he shows incredible patience in changing people. And because God does not force his love on anyone, the church is indeed a mixed bag of those who want to be changed by God and those who join but want to remain as they are. In the last chapter, we will come back to this tension between the 'already' and the 'not yet', this tension of a 'life between the times', between, on the one hand, God's decisive act for the salvation of humanity in the cross and resurrection of Jesus Christ and, on the other hand, the time of the final victory over the powers of sin and death at the end of history.

Because God's rescue plan is not completed, the church is a paradoxical reality that manifests both the life of God and human failing, even deliberate wrongdoing. Yet, because the power of the risen Christ and the Holy Spirit is present in the church, people can see in the church signs of deep love and unexpected grace. People are truly and profoundly changed, and, even while aware of their own failings, they may still experience the grace and love of God. Because of its failings, the church can never be identified with the kingdom or reign of God announced by Jesus Christ. Doing so might blind the church to its own sins and disobedience. Yet the church is a *sign* of the kingdom of God, of God's reign in the world, because in it we find people recognizing God as their King and Lord, calling and fighting for justice and peace as a sign of his reign.

7. The Christian Life

Christian belief and Christian living

Convictions change lives

It is slightly artificial to write a separate chapter on the Christian life. What Christians believe about how life should be lived is a direct consequence of what they believe about God and his project for humanity. That is why earlier chapters, in describing Christian beliefs, often referred to their implications for Christian living. Because God is immeasurably great and invites people to love him, they should love him above anything else. Because Christians believe in God's providence, they can fight against greed knowing that God will provide what they need. Because Christians believe that the earth on which they live is God's creation, they should respect and protect it. Because they believe that every person is created to be the image of God, they should treat everyone with equal respect and help them attain their God-given potential.

This close link between belief and behaviour is not just a Christian thing. In normal circumstances people act in accordance with their basic convictions about life, with what is sometimes called their 'worldview'. If you believe that your illness is caused by a physical defect, you will go to a doctor, who may diagnose your problem and prescribe a remedy. If you believe, rather, that your illness is caused by some spiritual force, you will go to a diviner, who may help you discover which spirit has been disturbed and what should be done to placate it. If you believe that happiness is defined by status and income, you will live accordingly, but if you believe that close relationships count most, you will have different priorities. You may believe that this life is one link in a long chain of rebirths, or that it ends with the decomposition of your body, or that after this life you will have to appear before the judgment seat of Allah, who will judge you according to the laws set out in the Qur'an. These convictions will lead to radically different lifestyles.

This is one reason why Christians believe that it is of utmost importance to work out what we should believe. It is sometimes thought that religious beliefs are rather marginal. As long as everyone tries to live a good life and seeks the best for others, discussions about religions only make things unnecessarily complex and risk leading to animosity, even war. The point is, however, that we cannot separate our religious convictions from our beliefs about what constitutes a good life and how we should aspire to it.

Some aspects of human behaviour, such as whether one prays or not, are obviously more directly related to religious beliefs than others, but religious beliefs also impinge on more 'secular' aspects of social life. If people believe that their ethnic group or race or caste has some privileged relation to their god and that they are therefore entitled to exploit people from other ethnic groups or castes, we can challenge them only by engaging with their understanding of who they are and of who others are. Christians will do that out of the conviction that every human being without distinction is made in the image of God. If people do not believe in God, they need to work out a different explanation of why they believe that such behaviour is unacceptable – if that is what they believe. They may of course simply state that all humans are equal, but on what basis do they say that? Because humans stand at the top of the evolutionary tree? Or do we need a better explanation? Many historians do in fact believe that modern convictions about unalienable human rights have their roots in Jewish and Christian convictions about the nature of the human person.

This is one of the reasons why Christians believe that both their worldview and the way of life they advocate is profoundly good news. Their worldview is good news because it says that there is a good God at the origin of the universe and because there is hope for the future. It is good news because it gives us a reason for treating everyone with respect. It is good news because it does not leave us in the dark about what life is actually about, so that human beings have to try to give meaning to their lives themselves. It says that life already has meaning and that far from *giving* meaning to it, the human task is to *discover* its meaning, a meaning that is far greater than people could ever give to it themselves: life is meant to be lived in a loving relationship with God, which makes it possible to flourish in the communities to which we belong and in the world in which we find ourselves.

God changes lives

For Christians there is an even closer relationship between their religious convictions and the way they live. Christian belief does not only relate to the Christian understanding of how life should be lived, because it gives a vision of what the world is like and how people should therefore live in order to flourish as they are meant to do. Christians actually believe that it is not enough just to present a picture of how people should live or to present a set of rules that tells them how to organize their lives. We have just indicated that people normally live in accordance with what they believe, but this is in fact too rosy a picture. Christians are deeply conscious of the fact that people are bound by forces that keep them from living the life they should live, even if they know they should change.

We discussed this earlier when talking about sin as an enslaving force (chapter 4). People may know that they should eat less and exercise more, but find it very hard to do so. Most people are aware of at least some of their vices, but find it incredibly hard to get rid of them. They know that it is often their own carelessness or lack of fidelity that makes it hard to develop good relationships with people around them, but find it hard to change. Christians also know that God is worth more than anything else in their lives, but they find that other persons, other things and other activities can so clutter their lives that it is hard to give God the pride of place he deserves.

There are two crucial elements of the Christian faith that deal with the feebleness of people's efforts to live up to what they believe their life should be. First there is the forgiveness of God. After each failure, people can come back to God, whom they have let down, and ask for forgiveness; and the Bible tells them that God is most willing to grant this request. This does not mean that forgiveness is cheap and that Christians can easily accept their failures and sins as if they do not matter too much. They matter to God, and as we saw in the last chapter, Christians believe that God let his own Son die on the cross to make forgiveness possible. Failures also matter to Christians themselves, for they know that each time they fail to live according to God's standards, they also miss out themselves. Not only do they miss out on the full joys of living, but they often cause pain to others arund them too. Yet forgiveness gives them the courage, every day, to leave these failures behind and start with a clean slate.

The second crucial resource that helps Christians deal with the enslaving power of sin is the gift of the Holy Spirit. We saw that Christians embrace the Holy Spirit as the gift of God who helps them change from the inside out. Sometimes Christians find that they are radically changed the moment they allow the Holy Spirit to transform them. Their lifestyle and relationships are revolutionized. Sometimes it is much more gradual, yet over the years they experience the healing power of the Holy Spirit that urges them along in their journey of learning to live renewed lives.

This is why many Christians find a number of other religions which primarily present a way of life proposed by prophets or enlightened people deeply unsatisfactory. Just showing people the path to liberation is not enough. This is poignantly expressed by Paul Williams, who embraced Tibetan Buddhism as a student and later became a lecturer and professor in Tibetan Buddhism. In November 1999, he wrote a letter to his friends telling them about his conversion to Christianity. In the book he wrote later about the main motives behind this conversion (*The Unexpected Way*, 2002) he indicated that one of the crucial difficulties he had with Buddhism was that it could not offer him any hope. If Buddhism were true, he could never hope to find the path to Enlightenment. Even after many decades on the Buddhist way, he was no closer to the goal. As he said, for him a religion could be satisfactory only if it was a religion not just for saints, but also for sinners. By himself he did not have the strength and saintliness to go the path the Buddha proposed. Christianity was much more realistic, because it offers forgiveness to sinners and a divine power that will help people change their lives.

Conversion

A change of direction

The need for a radical change of worldview and lifestyle helps us understand the central Christian notion of conversion. Following the example of Jesus, the Church calls people to conversion, to turn their lives around, away from the things that keep them from their God-given destiny and towards God himself. This is often understood as being closely related to what we have earlier called 'regeneration', that is, the moment someone enters into the life of the new creation. In a sense one could call conversion the outward side of regeneration, which is much more inward and can be only observed indirectly.

To Christians, conversion is firstly a change in life's basic orientation. It can be seen as a change of allegiance: whom does one consider Lord and King of one's life – the God we meet in Jesus, or someone or something else? It is also a change in where we seek our most fundamental security, and in what one finds supremely important – the pleasures offered by a hedonistic society, the love of one's spouse and children, the liberation of the soul proposed by the Buddha, the traditions of the ancestors, or rather the God of the Bible?

Conversion, secondly, entails not only a change in the basic orientation of life, but also in one's worldview, in one's most basic convictions about what the world is like, where history is going and what life is all about. The new orientation only makes sense if the corresponding worldview is believed to be true; if this God does indeed exist, if he is indeed the Creator of the world and the Master of history.

Thirdly, conversion consists of a change of lifestyle, for if one believes that this God is the Lord of the universe and of human destiny, one should try to obey him and seek to live according to his will for humankind. As we have seen, what people believe about the world has major implications for the way they live.

Fourthly, conversion implies that one identifies with a new community. When people become Christians, they do not usually leave their families and workplaces, but their relationships with these communities change. From then on their identity is more profoundly determined by the fact that they are now members of the Christian community, or rather by the fact that they now consider themselves children of God and members of the people or family of God.

Christians talk about conversion in two different, but related, senses. On the one hand conversion is talked about as a one-off event, the moment someone becomes a Christian, the moment one leaves a former life in order to make a new start as a follower of Jesus Christ. On the other hand Christians also speak about conversion as a daily aspect of the Christian life. In a sense, a Christian is never fully converted. In a world in which life with God is so counter-cultural, one needs constantly to turn back to God, constantly to refocus on God and constantly to leave behind those things which keep one away from being fully immersed in a life with God.

The Christian understanding of conversion would be misunderstood if one sees it as a great tour de force by the Christian who at a certain moment decides to completely turn their life around by a surge of willpower and inner strength. Christians believe that human beings enslaved by sin can never find the strength in themselves to completely change their lives. They believe that their salvation and the change in their lives happen 'by faith' and 'by grace' – to use two classic expressions. It is only possible by the grace of God because God gives his Holy Spirit who brings about this change free of charge as a gracious and undeserved gift. This gift is accepted 'by faith' and the person accepts it in faith, trusting that God will do in their life what this person cannot do themselves. Conversion is therefore first and foremost the act of placing one's faith and trust in Jesus Christ as Saviour of the world rather than in oneself or in anything else.

The need for conversion

Many non-Christians find this talk about conversion off-putting. In a world of many religions it is hard to accept one that asks others to join its community. In some societies this strains relationships between different religious groups. Talk about conversion also seems to suggest Christians consider themselves to have a better grasp of God and to be better people than those around, who presumably need converting. Finally, there is a strong feeling, particularly in Western countries, that we should allow everyone the freedom to work out for themselves how they want to organize their lives.

Christians do indeed believe that people need to make up their own minds. No-one should ever be forced to be a Christian, and most Christians today would look back with shame on those periods in history when force was used to bring people into the church. Freedom is an essential part of how Christians understand people's relationship with God; he wants them to accept freely his invitation to be his children. He does not look for grudging submission, but wants people to enter into a loving relationship with him.

The fact that God allows people freedom even when they choose not to serve him becomes clear in the well-known story told by Jesus usually called 'the parable of the prodigal son' (Luke 15:11–32). This is a story about a young man who no longer wants to live with his father and work for him. He asks for his share of his inheritance (despite the fact that his father was still alive!), goes away with it, squanders it in a distant land, and ends up entirely broke. The story is mainly known because of its ending, where it tells how the son comes back to the father to ask for forgiveness, and how the father gladly forgives him and welcomes him back into the family. Jesus told this story to teach his listeners about who God is: like this father, he longs for people to come back to him and is willing to forgive them even though they have hurt him so much.

The beginning of the story is equally remarkable, especially if we realize that it was told in a society where fathers had great authority over their children. It is amazing that the father in the story actually lets the son go and gives him his inheritance in advance, knowing that the son might squander it. Yet, like this father, God does not want humankind to serve and love him against their will. He does not want the type of relationship a master has with his slaves or a king has with his subjects. These can force people to obey. God therefore wants people to be his children and to love him freely. He therefore accepts it when people do not want to know him and decide to organize their lives without him. Yet, like the father in the parable, God waits and longs for his lost children to return to him.

This is one of the principal differences between Christianity and Islam. For Islam, the most basic image for understanding the relationship between God and humankind is that between a master and a slave or between a king and a subject. That may be an important reason why some strands in Islam are less hesitant to use economic or military force or manipulation to bring people within the fold of Islam and obedience to Allah. The relationship the God of the Bible looks for – the type of relationship a father has with his children or a lover has with his bride – can never be forced on people. That is why people should never be compelled to become Christians.

Yet although Christians believe that everyone should make

up their own minds about God and Jesus, they do not think that all choices are equal. Christians believe that some lifestyles are self-destructive or that they set people up for major disappointment. Because only God can give people true security in life, other life choices cannot remove a nagging sense of insecurity, even though they may be able to silence it for some time. Because people are created in order to find their fulfilment in a loving relationship with God, other lifestyle choices will leave people ultimately unsatisfied. Christians also believe that God is the only source of true life, and that a life without God is therefore headed for death, not just physical death, but eternal death. This is obviously a far-reaching and even disturbing thought that will need further elaboration in the next chapter.

Christians believe that not sharing their convictions about the ultimate meaning of life with others is a sign not so much of tolerance, but of indifference to the people around them. If one does indeed believe that encountering Jesus is the best thing one can do, one wants of course to share this belief with others and invite them to change the direction of their lives and embrace this Jesus and this faith.

It is not that Christians consider themselves better than others. They are just thankful that they have come to know this God and want to share this gift with as many people as possible. This is one of those gifts, like joy, gratitude, hope and love, that is not diminished when it is shared.

The whole of life and society

Religions and pseudo-religions

Christian belief has implications for how life in all its aspects should be lived. Christians believe that God's project for humanity touches on all areas of life. Given that he is our Maker, who is more able than he to tell us how life both individually and in society should be lived?

The fact that so far we have regularly referred to Christianity as a 'religion' may, therefore, be misleading. In modern Western society, there is a tendency to make a sharp distinction between the so-called public and private spheres in society. The public sphere should be guided by secular principles, it is often held. Religion should be relegated to the personal sphere of life, to what people do in their homes and to how they spend their time with likeminded people with whom they freely associate in their churches, synagogues, mosques or temples. Religion then has to do only with people's private relationship with God or some supernatural sphere, but should not be allowed to interfere with public life.

Particularly in the modern West, Christianity has often accepted the limited corner of life that society at large has wanted to allocate to it. Originally, and following its most fundamental convictions, however, Christianity cannot be understood as a religion in that limited sense. Christians believe that God is the Maker of the whole of life and that God's plan for the salvation of the world extends over all areas of life. Christian salvation consists not in a flight from this world, but in the salvation of the entire universe and society. Jesus' preaching of the kingdom of God showed that God has a project for life in its entirety. The resurrection of Christ as the beginning of the renewal of the entire creation indicates that there is nothing in this world that is beyond God's interest and power.

Christianity is not unique in presenting a project for all areas of life. The other major religions, such as Islam, Hinduism, Buddhism and traditional ethnic religions, would be similar in this respect. The idea that religion can be relegated to a particular sector of society is a typically modern and Western idea. It presumes that important parts of life are religiously neutral. It presupposes that how people do their work, how they organize their governments and how they entertain themselves have little to do with religious convictions. All major religions would contest that.

Christians would in fact want to argue that in claiming to know how to organize life and society, Western secular capitalism and consumerism have become a pseudo-religion. It may not resemble most religions, in that it does not believe in a god or gods – although neither does Buddhism. Yet it does resemble a religion in that it proposes a way to salvation and ultimate happiness: if you consume all you want and enjoy all the entertainment you can, you will find happiness. People may formulate the main tenets of this secular religion differently, but in all cases, Christians would believe this to be a lie: it is a pseudo-religion in that it promises the kind of fulfilment that only God can give.

The Christian claim that only God can satisfy the human quest for fulfilment is of course contested, and many Christians would be happy to enter into dialogue about why they believe their perspective to be true. Yet they also strongly contest the idea that modern secular values are in some strange way neutral and do not need to be scrutinized. Secular promises of what true life consists of need to be tested just as the Christian view in this matter does. Many Christians find these secular promises to be very superficial and flimsy. They would never have so much credibility were it not for the fact that they are constantly promoted by advertisers who want the public to buy their drinks, vacations, lifestyle products and so on, and persuade them that they contribute to the fulfilment of their lives.

Aspects of Christian ethics

Life in community

Christian ethical reflection – Christian reflection on how life should be lived – is, as we saw, closely related to Christian beliefs, to the Christian outlook on life and society. This does not, however, mean that Christian ethics are entirely unique and that there is no overlap between Christian ethics and different, non-Christian ideas on how life should be lived. Christians agree with many others who work for justice, peace and reconciliation, and values such as love, honesty and integrity are far from confined to Christians. Christians are also able to engage with others in ethical discussions about the issues that confront the societies in which they live.

From a Christian perspective, this readiness for dialogue and collaboration with others is possible because people all share a common humanity and because they all live in the same world. What makes life good can notonly be gleaned from the Christian Scriptures; fragments of it can also be picked up from carefully looking at the world and at what human life is like. Christians furthermore believe that God has given all human beings a conscience that gives them some sense of good and evil, right and wrong. Yet, as we saw earlier, Christians also believe that the human understanding of right and wrong is profoundly compromised by sin, and that the plan of God with the world is fully revealed only in the Bible. There are therefore many areas Christians and secular people or adherents of other religions deeply disagree about how life should be lived. Ongoing dialogue between the different groups that make up our societies is necessary.

In our discussion of the nature of human beings as the image of God, we saw that Christians understand humankind to be created for life in community. Human beings find their fulfilment as part of loving and caring communities. Modern individualism tends to regard the development of the *individual self* as a condition for the development of healthy relationships. This is reflected in the modern Western idea that everyone should be able to stand on their own feet, both financially and emotionally, and in the growing custom of people staying single for longer before committing themselves to long-lasting relationships.

Christians believe, by contrast, that *life in community* is the condition for the development and flourishing of the individual. This is most obvious in the early years, when children and young people need stable and loving families and communities in order to build up the self-confidence and moral capital with which they can later confront the world. Christians believe this to be equally true for later stages in life, when people can continue to flourish and grow if they are affirmed, loved and supported by others. The fact that some people do manage to grow strong in situations in which they can count on no-one but themselves doesn't make such situations healthy or desirable.

The communities in which people live are obviously not always loving and nurturing, and many people are profoundly damaged by the families in which they grow up and the communities that should nurture them. The possibility of such deep damage only underlines the importance of communities. The fact that life in community can be so profoundly nurturing and good, yet equally destructive, makes the ethics of life in community so important. Much of Christian ethics is precisely about how to establish healthy communities. It is about love, care, trustworthiness, responsibility, forgiveness and justice.

Marriage and sexual ethics

Because Christian ethics places such a high value on community and relationships, they also place a high value on marriage and emphasize sexual ethics. The marriage relationship is one that models the belief that people can become truly human only when they learn to appreciate and love someone who is both different and similar, and when they have the courage to care for this other person and to depend on him or her. In order for a marriage to flourish and become a true source of joy, one needs to be faithful and trustworthy, patient with the other and with oneself, willing to forgive and open to exploring unknown territory in the life of one's partner and of oneself. This is of course true of all profound relationships, but marriage exemplifies it in a special way because of its exclusive and lifelong nature. The stress in Christian ethics on marriage as a lifelong commitment to one person, and therefore Christian questioning of unmarried cohabitation and of easy divorce, need to be understood in this light. What is most valuable about marriage can grow only in a context of commitment and trust.

From a Christian perspective, one does not need to be married or happily married in order to be fully human. A number of Christian traditions have placed great value on the celibate life as one that can be especially dedicated to God and to other people. Yet one cannot be fully human in isolation. A solitary life, be it on a desert island or as a loner in a busy city, is a dehumanizing existence.

In this context it may be good to say a few words about the Christian understanding of sexuality, even though the limited exploration this chapter allows will only skim the surface of an area in which the Christian understanding is profoundly counter-cultural and therefore easily misunderstood. Modern Western society's attitude to sexuality is very ambiguous. On the one hand sexuality is considered hugely important. Publicity, television programmes and magazines tell us continuously that people need to be sexually active and that the pursuit of sexual experience is an essential, possibly the most essential, ingredient for happiness. On the other hand, this society encourages people, particularly young people and singles, to enter into sexual relationships fairly lightly. When the church calls for caution and says that proper limits are important because sexual experiences and relationships can also be deeply damaging, it is soon criticized for being unduly moralistic.

Christian ethicists from different persuasions consider this modern attitude both an overestimation and an underestimation of sexuality. It is an overestimation when it says that being sexually active is an essential ingredient of a happy life. Christians would say that sexual intercourse is a great gift of God, but that it points to something bigger. It is given in order to enjoy, celebrate and strengthen marital relationships, but the relationship of love and commitment which it celebrates is itself more important than the sex act. Furthermore, people can experience loving community in many different contexts in which sexual relationships would be inappropriate. A stress on sex easily draws the attention away from the meaning of true love and community, which is more essential to life than sex. That is also why a life focused on sex risks being deeply unfulfilling and always in search for more, while a life focused on love, community and true intimacy can be fulfilling and balanced even for someone who does not engage in sexual relationships.

Christian ethicists believe that the unwillingness to put any limits on sexual relationships between two consenting individuals reflects at the same time an underestimation of the importance of the sex act. Christians believe that what we do with our bodies is not peripheral to who we are, but reveals what we believe about ourselves. When I choose to engage in sexual intercourse only with my spouse, this reveals how much I value this committed relationship. It shows not only how important committed relationships are to me, but equally how important my body is to me and to my partner. As the former pope

John Paul II has underlined in his 'theology of the body', the Christian desire to limit sexual intercourse to lifelong committed relationships does not follow from a low view of sexuality, but rather from a high view. The way we use our bodies is a crucial part of how we view ourselves and our relationships.

Christian character

Our explorations so far have shown that Christian ethics is about much more than rules. It is true that even Christians have sometimes understood ethics to be primarily a list of do's and don'ts. That is why Christian ethics have often been considered to be a straitjacket that limits people in their lives. It should be clear by now that Christian ethics is also about values. It is because of the type of life, of relationships and of community that Christians value that they adhere to certain rules that make such a life possible and that protect it against behaviour and attitudes that might damage it. The rule that it is wrong to lie is so important because when people tell lies it is impossible to build communities based on mutual trust. The rule that one should not commit adultery reflects the positive value placed on sexuality as a unique celebration of the marriage relationship.

Christian ethics is not just about rules and values, but also about virtues and the development of character. In his moral teaching, Jesus Christ himself placed great stress on the attitude of the heart. Ethics is not just about not stealing, but about being satisfied with what one has and not desiring the possessions of others. Christian behaviour is not just about not committing murder, but about not hating people, not even one's enemies. It is not just about not committing adultery, but about not dwelling on one's desire for someone else's husband or wife (Matthew 5:27–28). In a famous passage, the apostle Paul describes what he calls 'the fruit of the Spirit', the sign that the Spirit is at work in people's lives, teaching them to live the life of the new creation, of the kingdom of God. This fruit of the Spirit consists of a list of virtues: 'love, joy, peace, patience, kindness, goodness, faithfulness, gentleness and self-control' (Galatians 5:22–23).

There are several reasons behind this stress on virtues and character, related to the different roles these virtues play in the Christian life. First of all, because Christian ethics is about what people value before it is about rules, it is also about what people love and what they are hooked on. In chapter 4, we noted that it is important to love things in accordance with their true value, and that is why Christians believe that one should love God more than anything else, and rich relationships with people more than material riches. Christian ethics encourages people to love and value what is truly worthy of love and to find joy in what gives the deepest joy. It is about not being content when God has so much more in store. It is about going for true joy and not being content with surrogates. It is also about not letting oneself be drawn away from what is truly worth enjoying and loving by pleasures that are only superficial or even damaging.

The development of Christian virtues and character is important, secondly, because the world in which Christians live does not make it easy to live a Christian life. In order to keep their priorities right, Christians need to distance themselves from what society around them promotes as most worthwhile, and they need to be willing to stick to it even when the rewards may not be immediate and when they face opposition. That is why virtues like self-control, courage and patience are so important. This is of course recognized by many non-Christians. One can attain what is truly worthwhile only when one is willing to be patient and learn to control oneself in the face of all those cheap promises of instant pleasure and gratification.

The maturing of Christian virtues is important, thirdly, so that one can become the sort of person that fits within the type of community that God envisages. God does not envisage a community in which people look first of all to their own interests, but rather one where they look out for ways to serve one another. God does not envisage the type of community in which people try to detach themselves from one another, as would be the Buddhist ideal, so that one can be merciful to others without being disturbed by other people's suffering. God envisages a community in which people have compassion, that is, they suffer with those who suffer and are joyful with those who experience joy. God does not want the type of community in which everyone knows and accepts his or her place in the social hierarchy or caste system, but one in which everyone considers others better than themselves. That is why virtues such as kindness, gentleness and humility are highly valued in the Christian community.

Virtue and character development is important, finally, because ethics cannot be limited to the just and equal treatment of everyone. Christians follow Jesus Christ as their great example. Jesus did not look for what was his due or his rightful share. Rather he came to serve others, even to the point of sacrificing himself and dying on the cross for the salvation of the world. If this Jesus is the example for Christian living, Christians need to develop the love for others which Jesus had. The 'love' that comes first in Paul's list of virtues is the self-sacrificial love that is willing to give oneself for others just as Jesus gave himself for the world. Such love can never be imposed by an ethical rule, but can only grow in people when, by the Spirit of Christ in them, they begin to resemble Christ more and more.

Social and political ethics

Given that Christian ethics touches on all areas of life, it also touches on Christians' life in the workplace and on their relationship with the political structures of the societies in which they live. Many Christians experience their work, whether on farms, or in factories, offices, schools or businesses, as part of their Christian calling. This is probably easiest for those in the caring professions, as the Christian faith places a high value on caring for those in need and on looking after and educating the next generation. Work has also been understood in the light of the 'cultural mandate' or 'creation mandate'. We did already discuss the Christian belief that, as the image of God, human beings have the mandate and calling to develop the resources of the earth so that they can feed their families, help those in need and honour God by what they do. This would be true not only for farmers and miners, but equally for artists and business people. All of these can in their own way see their work as done not only to maintain their families, but also to contribute to the well-being of the wider society and to honour God the Creator by making the most of the gifts he has given.

Christians do not always experience their jobs as good or meaningful. They may not have fulfilling jobs, having been excluded from the job market for one reason or another or because their work does not involve meaningful tasks. Others may be confined to a workplace that they experience as dehumanizing and in which they feel exploited. Others again may have work that may help them pay their bills, but that in itself is pointless rather than meaningful. Others again may feel that their society or situation forces them to do work that is destructive rather than beneficial for the community. Christian ethics for the workplace will want to help individuals to find or create a job that is both justly rewarded and worthwhile in the light of God's vocation to serve both him and humankind in the marketplace. It will also need to address wider social questions as to how Christians can contribute to building a society in which human labour helps to care for the Earth rather than exploit it, in which everyone has a good chance to find meaningful work, and in which work contributes to a better life for all, rather than bringing some people affluence at the expense of others.

This immediately leads to the question of what Christians believe about their involvement in the political structures of their nations. Christians have different attitudes to government, attitudes that often reflect their place in society. If Christians form a minority, sometimes even an oppressed minority, there may be little scope to contribute to or challenge their governments. In other countries Christians have a major influence in society, and there the question of what Christian belief implies for how a government should be run is less theoretical. Some believe that Christians should avoid all political functions and sometimes even government functions, and particularly avoid involvement in the military. Most Christians believe that it is good for Christians to be involved in the wider society and in their governments. God is the Master of all aspects of life, the Christian faith has major implications for how governments should be run and how they should use their power and resources.

This does not, however, mean that today's Christians would necessarily want to go back to a medieval type of society in which the church has a major influence in the government of states. They would not want to embrace a Christian version of the modern Islamic state, in which religious clerics determine many governmental policies. Much contemporary Christian thinking about the role of the Christian faith in modern societies would recognize the value of a proper separation of church and state. Both institutions, church and state, have their proper role in society, just as the structures of family and school do. Yet, because they believe that God is the Creator of everything that exists and that Jesus Christ is Lord over what governments do, Christians who work in the government or who are active in

politics want to follow Jesus Christ in those areas. They want
to further policies that reflect God's project for society, because
they believe that this is how humankind is meant to flourish
and how life is best organized.

Worship and prayer

At the end of this chapter it is important to note that all these
areas of Christian ethics can be correctly understood only when
seen in the light of how Christians understand their relationship
with God.

The Christian attitude towards the state, for example, is
determined by their attitude towards God. In history, we
constantly see how states have a tendency to become totalitarian
and make their own power absolute. Christians can never
allow a government to have absolute authority, because such
authority belongs only to God. That was one of the fundamental
tensions in the first centuries after Jesus Christ between the
early Christians and the Roman Empire. Christians refused to
sacrifice to statues of the Roman emperor. They were willing to
obey the government, but not to give it the honour and authority
that was due only to God. Worshipping God as the God of the
entire universe was therefore a politically charged act, and has
been so in many totalitarian states since then.

We have pointed out how for Christians their relationship
with God has major implications for their relationships with the
people around them. Because God himself is a relational God,
they know that true love is not some imaginary reality, but that
it is foundational to what life and even the universe itself is
about. They will want to model their own relationships on the
way God relates to them in self-giving love, in faithfulness and
in readiness to continue forgiving even after humankind had
so easily forgotten him and failed to appreciate his love and

forgiveness for what they are worth.

Christian worship and prayer also have major implications for how Christians relate to the material world around them. They accept and enjoy material gifts as God's blessing, but they try to avoid being trapped by material riches. They believe that their relationships with the people that are dearest to them are much more important, and that the love of God for them outweighs everything else. They believe that in prayer they can bring all their fears and desires to God, confident that he will know what they most need and that as their loving Father he will take care of them.

8. The Meaning and End of History

The meaning of history

God and history

We have pointed out several times that the Christian faith is a historical religion. The Christian faith is about a God who deals with people in the midst of history, gets involved with the often messy history of the people of Israel, and enters history himself in the person of Jesus Christ. God is a liberating presence within history, and as such he is working out the salvation of humankind in the course of it. Salvation is not about fleeing the world, but about living with God and having new hope in the midst of it.

The historical character of both the Jewish and Christian religions becomes clear when one considers the role of Abraham. The person of Abraham also plays an important role in Islam, and these three religions are often grouped together as the 'Abrahamic religions'. Yet there is a significant difference between the roles of Abraham in Islam on the one hand and in the Jewish-Christian tradition on the other. For Muslims, Abraham is first of all a prophet in the line of Adam and Enoch before him, and of David, Jesus and Muhammad after him. He is important because of his prophetic message that there is only one God, Allah, and that all should submit to him. In the Jewish and Christian traditions Abraham is important not so much because of the message he had for the world, but because of what God did in his life. God chose Abraham and his wife Sarah in order to begin a new people, the people of Israel. God was beginning a new history with the family and people of Abraham and Sarah, so that they might be a blessing for all humankind, not just by sharing the message of salvation, but because the Messiah, the future liberator and king who would be the saviour of all humankind and even of the universe, would be born from this nation. If Abraham is commended in the New Testament, it is not for his prophetic message, but for his faith, because he trusted in God and believed that God would indeed make him a great nation and a blessing for all the nations.

Later in the history of their nation, the people of Israel continued to experience God's involvement with them. A point of reference to which they always came back was the 'exodus' out of Egypt where the descendants of Abraham had ended up as slaves. After a long and perilous journey through the desert of the Sinai peninsula, he gave them the country which is currently called Israel where they were allowed to settle and live in freedom. Yet the peace and freedom did not last, and the people of Israel were almost continually bullied by the surrounding people. After many centuries, the people of the northern region were taken away into captivity, and later still the remaining southern part of the nation was conquered by the Babylonian armies, which destroyed their capital city, Jerusalem, and the Temple of God that was built there. The remnant of the population was taken into exile in the city of Babylon, in present-day Iraq. According to the Bible, this exile was in fact a punishment from God, because Israel did not live up to its calling to be his special people. Being in a covenant relationship with God, they were supposed to obey his commandments and show the world how good it was to live with this God. Because they were his chosen nation, they were called to live differently and because they didn't, they ended up in exile.

The prophetic messages given to Israel made it increasingly clear that it would not do for God simply to bring them back to their own country. They would be able to live the new life that God wanted them to live only once they had undergone a much more radical change. The prophets therefore spoke more and more, and with increasing clarity, about such a radical change in the future, when God would begin an entirely new episode in the history of Israel and even in the history of the world. In that day, God would not only liberate his people from their oppressors; he would make a new covenant with them, and give them his Holy Spirit, who would change them radically from the inside out, so that from then on they would serve God wholeheartedly. They would be a light for the nations, and the whole world would be able to see and experience the salvation of the God of Israel. The later prophets even speak about cosmic changes which would take place, in which the entire universe would be renewed and in which the dead would rise to a new life.

Jesus Christ as the centre of history

Christians believe that this decisive moment when God began a new relationship with Israel and humankind came with Jesus Christ. It came, however, in a way entirely different from what the people at the time expected. In many respects history went on as it always did. Israel was still oppressed by its enemies and people continued to die. Hatred and strife were a reality. Yet the followers of Jesus believed that in an important sense the end of history had already come. Christians believe that Jesus Christ rose from the dead on the third day after his body had been placed in the grave. He experienced the resurrection they were expecting at the end of time. This they take as the decisive proof that Jesus really conquered the power of death.

The followers of Jesus had heard him announce that his death and resurrection would inaugurate the long-expected new covenant. The risen Jesus Christ then gave them the Holy Spirit, another gift promised for the end of history and the most central gift of this new covenant, this new relationship between God and humankind. The first Christians had a powerful experience of the Spirit of God urging them to renew their lives and giving them an entirely new sense of the nearness of God, who now lived in them. They also experienced the healing power of the Spirit in their lives as a liberation from the destructive forces that had for so long kept the world in their grip.

This gave Christians an entirely new understanding of the time in which they were living – an understanding which distinguished them from those Jews who did not accept Jesus Christ as their Messiah and who therefore continued to wait for the end of history. For Christians, the end of history had already come in Jesus Christ. Or rather, the end of history had begun, had been inaugurated. In another sense, history still continued. The powers of death, hatred, sin and destruction were still active in the world. But the resurrection of Jesus Christ and the gift of the Holy Spirit showed that the end-time had decisively begun. The fact that the reality of the new world – the Holy Spirit and the power of the risen Jesus Christ – was already present among them made them confident that the rest would also come. God has, after all, already made the 'down-payment' on the world to come.

This is why, for Christians, Jesus Christ is the linchpin of history. They even divide history into the years 'before Christ' (BC) and 'after Christ' or more precisely 'in the year of the Lord' (in Latin: Anno Domini or AD). Christians look back to God's decisive actions in Jesus Christ and believe on that basis that they have a well-founded hope when they look to the future and expect God to act again, this time to establish justice and peace on the entire earth and to even renew the entire universe.

The resurrection and the meaning of history

The Christian understanding of where they live in history, where they come from and what they expect for the future, deeply influences how Christians live their daily lives here and now. This is true not only for Christians, but for everyone. What people expect for the future determines how they live now. If it doesn't, we may want to ask whether they truly believe what they say they believe. People who believe that after death they will join the spirits of their ancestors will live differently from those who believe that after this life they will enter another cycle of rebirth, which will be determined by the *karma* built up in their current life. People who believe that the only future is a future for the coming generations on this planet, will live differently from those who believe in an afterlife in a spiritual world beyond.

When we examine different religious and ideological perspectives on the end of life, there seem to be two basic options. Some believe in a future for this earth, in a better world to come for the next generations, possibly even a utopia or ideal world. Yet they won't have a part in that world, because they will be dead and gone by the time it comes. Others believe in a spiritual existence beyond death, in which they can attain a new and blessed state of being. But that makes the future of the physical world less important, or important only in so far as it helps others to leave this world properly in order to enter a Paradise or *nirvana* beyond. Either people have hopes for this world, but do not expect to share in it; or they have hope for themselves and feel they have to renounce the world and their bodily existence in order to attain it.

The decisive reality which makes this dilemma unavoidable is of course the reality of physical death: when people die, there is either a future for them in a spiritual world beyond or for this physical world without them. It is only belief in a bodily resurrection at the end of time that provides a way out of this dilemma. This belief in a resurrection at the end of time is also found in important strands of Jewish thinking. Because Jews believe that God is the Creator of the world, they came to believe that God will remain faithful to what he has made and also to the human beings he has brought into this world. That is why he will raise them to new life at the end of time.

In the Christian tradition this belief in the resurrection has become much more central because of the belief that God raised Christ from death and that Jesus is therefore the sure sign that the resurrection of all will follow. Understandably, this is a belief which many non-Christians find really hard to accept. They may even find it hard to imagine that others can truly believe it. It seems so counter-intuitive in a world in which death is an ever-present and inevitable reality. It is important to see how Christians can make sense of it in the light of their belief in creation. Even such a big thing as the resurrection is not beyond the power of God, who made the world in the first place. It is furthermore possible for Christians to believe it because they believe that God raised Jesus from the dead. When prompted, many of them will even give reasons why they think they have good historical grounds to believe that Christ's resurrection truly happened.

Living in the expectation of a resurrection and the renewal of the universe at the end of time has major implications for how Christians live now. It means that life in this body is truly important: it is a gift from God, for which he has a future. It is even more important than it would have been had this life been the only thing there is, for, rather than heading for personal or collective extinction, people are destined for an eternal future. And as we will see later, Christians believe that the way people live their lives has a significance for eternity, for the new life that follows on the other side of physical death.

A new heaven and a new earth

It is true that not all Christians live with the same expectations. They have often placed more stress on the expectation of life in heaven than on a future resurrected life on a new Earth. There are several reasons for this change from the New Testament expection of a resurrection at the end of time to an expectation of a spiritual heaven.

Firstly, most Christians realize that they may no longer be alive when God re-establishes all things at the end of history. Most Christians furthermore expect those among them who die before the end of time to be taken up to heaven, the realm of God. There their souls are allowed to rest in the presence of God and wait for the resurrection of the body and the renewal of the entire universe at the end of time. The expectation of this more immediate existence beyond physical death became more and more important, particularly so in situations where Christians are oppressed or even martyred, or where life in general is very uncertain because of violence, war, extreme poverty or disease.

In such circumstances it is a huge encouragement that even after one's physical death, one's soul or spirit is safe with God and will experience his presence and joy in a new way. This perspective often became so important that it almost replaced the expectation of the resurrection at the end of time.

A second reason why the expectation of a new heaven and a new earth became replaced by the hope of heaven was the general influence of classical Greek styles of thought in the church. Classical Greek philosophy tended to undervalue the body and its existence in history, and promoted the idea that a purely spiritual existence would somehow be better than an eternal life on earth, even on a renewed earth. This attitude to the body also led to a lack of care both for what people do with their bodies and for how they treat the environment.

The belief in the resurrection of human beings in a new bodily existence at the end of time has, however, always been a central aspect of the Christian faith. There is an increasing awareness among Christians today that it is inappropriate to think of their future eternal existence as an angel-like life in a spiritual heaven in which those who are saved will do nothing but join in with the angelic choirs. There is also an increasing awareness that if God is going to be faithful to the earth and to human beings as whole beings, including their bodies, this should have major implications for how they live in this world. It gives them hope for the earth and also a sense of responsibility for how they treat the environment.

The relationship between this world and the world to come is a complex one in Christian thinking. In fact, the Bible does not say much about what this future existence will be like, except that those who will rise will be like Jesus Christ after his resurrection. He was after all the 'first-fruits' of the new creation. This gives some pointers to what this future existence will be like. It shows that there will be continuity between this world and the world to come. Jesus rose from the dead into a new life with a body identical to the one he had before. This shows that God remained faithful to his former physical existence, which God wanted to save and renew. Some Christians therefore believe that there will be an important continuity between this world and the world to come: it is the current universe that will be renewed.

When Christians look to the risen life of Jesus, they see at the same time a radical change. The risen Jesus Christ had a new existence which was no longer subject to death and decay. In this new existence he lives for eternity, and his followers may join him in it. Jesus' existence did not seem to be bound by the same physical boundaries as ordinary human existence, and Jesus indicates elsewhere that human relationships will change radically. People will, for example, no longer get married. There will be human relationships, for there will be a people of God and the relationships among them will presumably be intensified rather than cut off. This community and the new relationship with God may well be so intense and fulfilling that special relationships such as marriage may no longer be needed. In general, Christians tend not to speculate too much about the nature of this life to come. It will be a life in which God will fill their entire existence and in which all that is most precious in this current life will find its fulfilment. There will be harmony among humankind, harmony within the universe and peace with God. Knowing that is enough.

In the new world, there will no longer be a separation between heaven as the realm of God and the earth as the place where his will is so often disobeyed. In that sense 'the new heaven and the new earth' about which Scripture speaks will not be two places, but rather one. Heaven will come on earth, and the new earth will be the place where God will be present as never before and where his love will penetrate all that exists.

This may be a final reason why Christians sometimes talk more about heaven than about the renewal of the earth: their deepest longing is to be united with God, to experience the presence of God with an intensity that is not yet possible in the current world. They believe that this presence of God is characteristic of heaven and that it will characterize the world to come.

Living between the times

Life for Christians today is therefore characterized as what is sometimes called 'life between the times'. Their lives are inspired and renewed because of what God has done in the past, in the cross and resurrection of Jesus Christ and in the gift of the Holy Spirit at Pentecost. Because of that, they live new lives and are in an important sense part of the new creation, of the redeemed world which was inaugurated with Christ. On the other hand, they still live in the midst of the old and unredeemed world and look forward to the final redemption of all things at the end of history.

This age between the times can therefore be described as the age of the Holy Spirit. During this period in the history of God with humankind, God works particularly through the Holy Spirit. God has given this personal presence of himself, who is at the same time a power that changes and renews people, so that they become more like Jesus Christ. An important feature of this work of the Holy Spirit is that he does not force himself on people. This was equally true of God's presence in Jesus Christ. God allows people to accept this offer of his love and salvation, but equally he allows people to reject it. In the case of Jesus, this became acutely apparent when humankind did not want to hear his message and ended up killing him on a cross. In the same way, God does not force himself on people by his Holy Spirit. His Holy Spirit speaks to people when the good news about Jesus Christ is proclaimed and when he urges them to change their lives. But people are free to reject this good news, and many do so.

The fact that many people do reject the good news of Jesus Christ is for Christians not a sign of its weakness. It is part of how God relates to people. He could make himself known with all his power and might so that his presence and power would be unmistakable and so that no-one could reject him. He does, however, want people to accept his love freely, because they want to. That is why God wants to convince them with his message, his love and the gentle urgings of his Holy Spirit. God wants to be the Father of humankind and wants people to live as his children. Such a relationship of love and respect can never be exacted, but only freely embraced. That is why God currently works among humankind by his Holy Spirit so as to make it possible for them to experience his love and salvation without having it forced on them.

Christians believe that at the end of time God will indeed reveal his power unmistakably, but that this will also be the time when current history ends and it will no longer be possible freely to accept the grace and love of God. At that time, it will become clear where everyone then living or who has ever lived stands in relation to God – whether they will be with those who reject God's offer or those who accept it.

This also means that the age between the times is for Christians an age of great opportunity. It is therefore also the age of mission. 'Mission' is a term Christians use for all activities that the Christian community undertake in order to make God's love and plan of salvation known to the world. This includes all their efforts to make something of this love and salvation visible in the care that is given to people in need, and in the fight for justice, for a world that looks more like the world as

God intended it to be. Christians believe that when they are involved in such mission activities, they are in fact involved in the mission of God himself, who is actively at work to draw people to himself, into the circle of his love.

The last judgment

Putting things right

The expectation of the last judgment at the end of time has traditionally been very prominent in Christian beliefs about the end of the world. It has been pictured in many paintings and stained-glass windows in ancient churches and cathedrals. At the top one sees an image of a person representing God or Jesus as judge. Near the bottom the artist has usually depicted graves that are opened, with the dead in them being brought back to life. These pictures also show how humankind is separated into two different groups. At one side are those who are dragged down into hell by the devil and his demons. The other group is taken by the angels of God into Paradise or heaven, where they will live redeemed lives for ever.

The fear induced by this type of picture has made many people extremely uncomfortable. It may be reminiscences of such fears that provoke reactions such as the 2008 atheist poster campaign on London buses. For a number of weeks, buses carried the slogan: 'There's probably no God. Now stop worrying and enjoy your life.' The slogan seems to assume that many people are Christians, because it plays on the fear of a final judgment. They cannot really enjoy their lives now, because they fear that God is going to punish them for all their misbehaviour by letting them burn for eternity in hell.

Many contemporary Christians are probably slightly

bewildered by the suggestion that they are believers out of fear and that their beliefs stop them from enjoying life. There have been periods in history when the church has used the fear of hell to keep people under control and make them toe the line. However, most people who become Christian nowadays probably do so because they find in their relationship with God a much deeper joy than they were able to find elsewhere.

That does not, however, discredit the importance of the Christian belief in a judgment at the end of time. This belief is not linked with any one way of picturing it. This is true for all images, in art forms such as novels and paintings, by which Christians try to express the reality they encounter in their Scriptures. They need to relate to it in a manner that makes sense to them, yet the images they produce are not necessarily equally helpful to all. This is also true of the way Christians depict judgment. Yet, though it can be pictured in different ways, Christian belief in the last judgment is linked closely with two crucial aspects of the Christian understanding of the world and the Christian hope for the future.

The expectation of a final judgment, firstly, entails that the God of the universe will in the end destroy all the powers of evil and put things right again. The last judgment could, with a nod to Tolkien's *Lord of the Rings* trilogy, be called 'the return of the King'. God is the rightful King of his universe. Humanity, which has lived for so long as though he did not exist, will have to recognize his authority. This does mean that this world does not belong to the oppressors, whether the great oppressors who control the power of entire states, multinationals or media empires, or the small oppressors who abuse vulnerable people in their immediate environment. Christians believe that the great and small bullies of this world will not have the last word. They will appear before the judgment seat of God, where they will have to give an account of their behaviour. Those who have been oppressed will be restored and go free. The final judgment will mean that God will finally put things right.

The basis of judgment

The expectation of a final judgment, secondly, means that there will be a separation between those who will spend eternal life with God in the new creation and those who will be excluded from that new world. This is one of the Christian convictions that has received the most vehement critical reactions. Christians themselves do not always find it easy to understand how God can exclude people from this new world. They believe after all that God is loving. He is willing to forgive and welcome even the greatest sinner and most evil person. Christian thinkers have given different answers to these objections, answers that arise out of some of the deepest Christian convictions.

Christians would first of all want to underline that God is not only loving and forgiving, but also just. More precisely, God's love and forgiveness can be understood only in relationship to his justice. The love of a God who is not just and does not oppose injustice and evil would be a soft love that couldn't make a serious dent in this world where injustice is so rampant. A God who truly wants the best for this world needs to fight evil and injustice. God's justice is part of his love. Because he is a just and loving God, he has to condemn evil. There is no place for injustice in his new creation.

Forgiveness itself doesn't even make sense unless evil is called what it is. If we just let evil behaviour continue without ever commenting on it, we are not forgiving, but rather simply indifferent to evil. Forgiveness is possible when evil is recognized for what it is and when people are willing to give up the evil they have done. Forgiveness is about repairing relationships. Suppose that someone has done serious harm to one of my children. The person could probably never make up for the pain caused to my child and me, but I may still be able to forgive him and our relationship may still be repaired. But if this person wants to continue to harm my children, I may show a forgiving attitude, but I need to protect my children and will not allow this person near them. In the same way, people can be restored to a right relationship with God only when they are willing to ask for forgiveness and when they are willing to let go of the evil they have done. Given all it has cost God, he will not let evil destroy the new world he is going to establish.

Finally it is important to realize that Christians believe that God himself is the centre of the new creation. The world to come is not about 'pie in the sky when we die', some general sense of happiness that all would want to share in. Who would not want a piece of the giant cake of heaven or Paradise? Yet heaven is not like a piece of cake that, when offered, anyone with a good appetite would want to accept. Heaven, or the new creation, is all about God. It is about an eternal, loving relationship with God of an intensity that people have never known before.

For people who have sought God all their lives or for those who discovered later in life that they truly need God more than anything else, this is of course the best thing that can ever happen. Yet if people have filled their lives with things other than God, or have been fleeing from God, or fighting God, eternal life with God can hardly be a blessing. They can continue to flee from him or, alternatively, radically turn their back on their old lives, ask for forgiveness and from then on give God his place as the love of their lives. But eternally living without God in God's presence is simply no option and for people who desire to live without him, the new creation would definitely be an impossible place to be. The English author C. S. Lewis portrayed this succinctly in his novel *The Great Divorce*, written as a parable of heaven and hell: in the end, there will only be two sorts of people. There will be people who say to God 'Your will be done.' They will joyfully enter the life God has prepared for them. And there will be those to whom God says: 'Your will be done. If you do not want to live with me, you will need to live eternally outside my presence.'

That is what Christians believe to be the alternative to eternal life with God. It is true that they differ significantly in their understanding of what hell is. Some will take the biblical pictures of 'a lake of fire' literally and believe it to be a place where people will suffer excruciating pain eternally. Others would see the biblical images of hell as just that, images. The essence of hell is that it is where God is absent and where people experience the eternal deception of having chosen a life that is no true life but rather leads to death. Others again would say that hell is just that: death, or more radically, eternal death, the eternal destruction or annihilation of those who have chosen a life without God.

However hell is understood, Christians shudder at the fact that people's destructive choices can lead to lives being lost for ever. Christians recognize this to be the flipside of the belief that the love of God is both the source and the goal of human existence: true life can be found only in relationship with God. It is the flipside of the belief that God invites people into an eternal relationship with himself, the kind of relationship that a bridegroom has with the love of his life, or a father with his children. Such love can only be accepted freely. God takes humankind so seriously that he does not force himself on them, but even accepts their 'no', and the pain of rejection that that causes him.

Conclusion: Christian Belief in a Global Village

Globalization

Over the pages of this book it has become evident that the Christian belief that Jesus Christ is the Saviour of humanity and the Lord of the universe can be expressed in many different ways as it relates to ever new cultural contexts. Today this becomes clear as never before as we encounter Christianity in such varied forms in different parts of the globe. For many centuries, most people lived in relatively stable and uniform cultural environments and scarcely realized how different people can be. People have always told stories about distant pasts and faraway countries where life was so different from what they considered normal. But that's the point: they looked on those other cultures as exotic and strange. They weren't a real challenge to how they saw themselves, because the way they lived was just the way things were and how they were supposed to be.

All this has been changed by the forces of globalization. Globalization is a technical term for the process by which societies in different parts of the world become increasingly interrelated and dependent on one another. This process has been going on for centuries, but accelerated significantly in the course of the last century. Through modern media like television and the internet, we now know much more about how people live elsewhere. Through increasing travel, and even more through the migration of enormous groups of people across the globe, we can now gain a firsthand experience of other cultures and have neighbours in our street who live quite differently from us. Because we recognize so much in other people that is similar to ourselves, they are no longer just exotic strangers in a world that doesn't impact ours. Yet because they are at the same time so different, we realize that life can be lived in many different ways and that people make sense of life in radically different manners.

In many people, this has led to what the sociologist Peter Berger calls 'the vertigo of relativity'. When everyone around us lives in the same way and experiences life similarly, it feels as if that is just what life consists of. But when we meet people who experience life differently, this forces us to make up our mind about what we consider life to be. When we encounter a range of radically different ways of life, as we do in our global village, this can lead to an experience of vertigo. There are so many options that one's head may start spinning, and this can easily and understandably lead to the belief that all perspectives are equally valuable, and that everything we believe is relative to where we stand in life and to the culture in which we are born.

Negotiating cultural vertigo

Christians today relate their faith not only to different cultural contexts, but also to the cultural phenomenon of multiculturalism itself, to the fact that so many cultures find themselves in close proximity to one another. Every religion or worldview today must relate to this context, simply because people have to work out how to live in this multicultural world. In addressing these questions today, Christian thinkers have discovered that their tradition provides rich resources for doing so.

First of all, Christianity has itself from the very beginning been a globalizing movement. From the church's birth at Pentecost onwards, the followers of Jesus went out to the four corners of the world to share the message of Jesus Christ. They believed, after all, that the one Creator of the whole of humanity had made himself known in Jesus Christ, and that God's plan of salvation encompassed the whole creation. All the nations were therefore invited to put their trust in Jesus Christ. Christianity, then, provides an alternative globalizing movement to the Western colonization of the world, first through military power and later through the spread of Western capitalism and consumerism.

Secondly, the worldwide proclamation of the Christian faith is a movement that need not suppress local cultural differences, because this faith can be expressed in many cultural forms. It is true that Christians have a tendency to impose their own variety of the Christian faith on others, be it in the form of the Latin Eucharist or by exporting the televised messages of American evangelists. Yet in itself Christianity is well placed to respect rather than suppress cultural differences. As we saw earlier, the Christian faith has from its very beginning been communicated in different languages and different cultural forms, and in this way it has allowed different societies to flourish in new ways, each bringing its unique contribution to the worldwide community of the one new people of the one God.

In the third place, the Christian message does not affirm every aspect of every cultural context. Christians believe that the way people live and organize their societies reflects their efforts to live without God and often at the expense of other people, particularly weaker groups in society. The Christian message can therefore be highly critical of cultures, including cultures that call themselves Christian. All fall short of what God intends for human life.

This often seems arrogant to non-Christians. Where do Christians get the right to judge others about how they should live? In order to understand this side of the Christian attitude towards cultures, we must first recognize that most of us in fact believe some aspects of other cultures to be unhelpful or even dangerous. When the British colonized India, they prohibited the cultural custom of burning widows along with the bodies of their deceased husbands. When genocide is being perpetrated in some part of the world, many people feel that it is legitimate for the international community to intervene in order to protect vulnerable groups. When a government feels free to torture minorities, other governments may put pressure on it to respect basic human rights. People do not ask whether widow-burning, genocide or torture is consistent with different cultural outlooks, but simply condemn it and feel that people deserve to be protected from such behaviour. Being uncritical of whatever is going on in other cultures may be a sign of indifference to the suffering of others just as much as a sign of cultural respect.

Where do people derive the criteria that allow them to criticize such cultural practices? They come from a specific outlook on society, whether a Western understanding of universal human rights, a Muslim understanding of *sharia* law, a Buddhist understanding of compassion for the suffering, or some other perspective that leads to compassion and to indignation at forms of suffering and injustice one finds particularly intolerable. Christians believe that God's revelation in Jesus Christ of his plan for humanity is the best starting-point for cultural criticism. The Christian understanding of humankind as created in the image of God provides a key to understanding what human flourishing is meant to look like. It therefore provides Christians with a key to understanding the type of freedom that is most important: the opportunity for everyone to live as God wants them to, and to flourish as God invites them to.

Navigating the waters of religious pluralism

The problem remains that the Christian answer to what it means to be human is only one among others. The idea that human beings are essentially consumers who flourish when they enjoy as much luxury consumption and entertainment as possible is an alternative answer, as is the idea that human beings are just a product of evolution, which will be forced to muster its best resources in the fight of all against all for the survival of the fittest. The claim that all individual human beings will be able to choose their personal style of self-development when their fundamental rights are protected is a third answer widespread in the West. Different religions provide their own answers too, such as the Muslim answer that centres on obedience to Allah, the Buddhist answer based on the search for spiritual enlightenment, and the Hindu answer offering liberation through multiple reincarnations. How should people navigate these waters of a pluralist world of religious and pseudo-religious options? This is another aspect of life in the multicultural global village in which Christians live and in which they need to find their place, just like everyone else.

A popular modern way of approaching the diversity of religious traditions is to see all of them as different paths to one spiritual reality, as different expressions of a mystical experience of one divine reality. Because this reality is beyond human speech, people can talk about it in words that sound contradictory. Some may talk about a personal God, others about an impersonal divinity, some about many gods, others about a single divine force that penetrates the entire universe. This approach definitely sounds attractive, because it seems to be a neutral one that does not force us to choose among the religions, but allows us to accept them all as imperfect efforts to capture the one divine reality which surpasses all human words.

One could question, however, whether this approach to religion is truly neutral. It says in fact that some religious forms are normative, particularly mystical forms that worship a divine reality beyond words. At the same time it assesses most religious forms as immature expressions of this fundamental religious core. Muslims, who believe that Mohammed is the seal of the prophets, Christians, who believe that Jesus is in a unique sense the Son of God, and African Traditional Religions, which concentrate their efforts on maintaining good relationships with the ancestor spirits, are said to have not yet understood what religion is about. The problem is that these convictions are central for the adherents of these religions. Most of them would not agree that mystical experience is the best way to relate to the divine. This modern approach therefore ends up condemning most religious practices rather than embracing them. The approach furthermore erases the real differences between religions. These are not secondary, because they profoundly influence how people see themselves and how they live. People who believe that true life is found in obeying the law of God live differently from people who believe that true life is found in loving God. People who believe that they should detach themselves from the world and those around them live differently from people who believe that life in its fullness is found in enjoying the world and those around them.

As an alternative approach to the variety of religions that respects their real differences, others have proposed that we should simply give up on the search for one universal religious truth. This position could be labelled 'postmodern', and is associated with a number of thinkers who have criticized the search for a universal religious truth as a typically modern Western ideal. These postmodern thinkers would understand the various religions as different cultural products, different ways in which societies and peoples make sense of reality and organize their lives. They are not meant to express a universal truth that is valid for all. They are valid only for the adherents of these particular religions. Islam is true for Muslims as Christianity is for Christians, because their respective rituals, stories and customs help each of these groups organize their lives and worlds.

This again is not a neutral approach to religion. Equally, the postmodern approach does tell what is right and wrong in the religions. It is very critical of the self-understanding of those religions that believe that God was there before they believed in him. For Muslims, Christians and many others, their religions are not about human beings organizing their world, but about humans accepting that God has organized their world for them and that they must recognize God for who he is. They believe that people must leave their own man-made religions and gods for the one true God. In telling what is right and wrong in the different religions, modern and postmodern approaches aren't any different to religious approaches to religious pluralism.

Most religions also have some sense of how and why other religions are partially true and false. Muslims would, for example, say that Christianity is partially valid in so far as it recognizes Jesus as a prophet of the one true God, but that it is wrong in making him the Son of God, for the true God cannot have a son. Hindus, on the contrary, would say that Christians may be right in recognizing Jesus as a son of God who revealed God to them, but that they are entirely wrong in supposing that God can have only one son or would come to earth at just one single time and place. Their God presents himself in many *avatar*s and can be known through many different mediators.

Jesus Christ as the way, the truth and the life

Christians are not immune from their cultural contexts. A number of Christians, particularly in the West, have therefore shared the two types of answers to religious pluralism sketched above. Some have regarded Christianity as one cultural expression of a universal religious experience. Others have seen Christianity as the way their tradition and community make sense of life and the world, and therefore is true only for the Christian community. Yet these approaches are hard to square with some of the most fundamental Christian beliefs, such as the belief that religious experience is not the best way to God, but rather the way God himself has opened up in Jesus Christ. It also clashes with the fundamental belief that Christianity is not about how Christians organize their lives and give themselves hope, but how God himself acted for the salvation of humanity, precisely because humankind is not able to save itself or give itself a hope that holds firm in the face of evil and death.

Both of these approaches have the advantage, of course, that they appear to share a neutral attitude towards all religions. But, as we saw in the last section, neutrality is not possible. One always looks at religion from a particular perspective, be it a modern or postmodern Western perspective, a Christian, Muslim or Hindu one, or whatever religious one. There is no way of avoiding the question of whether there is a God, what this reality might be like, and whether and how such a divine reality makes itself or himself known in one or in many religions. One cannot even remain agnostic, because a position which says that we cannot know whether God can be known, or what the divine might be like, claims at least some knowledge about the divine: it says that the divine cannot make itself known and that if it could, it would not be worth searching for it. Christians would of course disagree. One has to make up one's mind about the many religious claims.

In traditional Christian faith, belief in Jesus Christ is central not only to its understanding of God and of human identity, but equally for its understanding of the world of the many human religions. God's revelation in Jesus both affirms and criticizes the religions. On one hand it affirms the religious quest for God. The fact that there are so many understandings of the divine could easily lead to the conclusion that the idea that God can be known is just a chimera and that humankind needs to learn to live without God. If God makes himself known in Jesus, this means that the human search for God, for a security beyond the fleetingness of this world, for a meaning in life beyond all the things in this world that can never satisfy, and for a life beyond the ten, forty or ninety years between birth and death, is not in vain. The deep longing people experience for something like God, and the profound desire for a harmony and love that seem impossible in this broken world, are then not by-products of blind evolution, but planted in them by God himself.

On the other hand, if God's plan for the world is revealed in Jesus of Nazareth, this also implies a criticism of human religion. It shows that all human efforts to know God have provided only very limited and often contradictory results. Under its own steam, humanity will simply not be able to understand God adequately. It also shows that people are often too easily satisfied with their limited understandings of God and have often come up with fairly limited images of God that bring him down to a level the human imagination can handle. Finally, it shows that human beings have often used religion to protect their own interests rather than as a tool to serve the weak and oppressed. Oppression has even been legitimized by an appeal to religion, when it claims that God himself allocates people their place in society as members of a lower class or caste. Christians have not been immune from using religion for their own advantage, as a support for the lives they have designed for themselves rather than as a call to radically change their lives and live as God wants them to. Christians believe, therefore, that all religions thus stand in urgent need of Christ, as the fulfilment of all that is true and good in them, yet also to purify them from all abuse.

As with all Christian beliefs, this Christian understanding of human religion and the religious quest for God stands or falls with what Christians believe about Jesus. According to the Gospel of John, Jesus calls himself 'the way and the truth and the life' (John 14:6). He presents himself as the place where the truth of God can be known in person, as the way to God and as the fullness of life itself. One can make up one's mind about Christian belief only if one makes up one's mind about this Jesus Christ.

Glossary

Age of Reason
The eighteenth-century movement in Western European culture characterized by great confidence in human reason.

agnostic
Someone who holds the conviction that it is impossible to prove or disprove whether there is a God and difficult to know what such a God might be like.

Anglican Church
The state church in England, which, through its missionary efforts, was also planted in many former British colonies.

avatar
A term from Hinduism for one of the many appearances of the god Vishnu in human form, the most important of whom is Krishna.

baptism
The ritual by which a person – as an infant or later in life – becomes a member of the church through being sprinkled with or immersed in water.

Bible
The commonest name for the collection of texts Christians consider to be their Holy Scriptures and therefore as foundational for their understanding of God.

born again
A term used of someone who has begun a new life as a Christian. It has also come to designate a particular movement within the Protestant tradition which places a particular stress on the need to be born again.

caste system
A social system, particularly strong in India, which is based on the Hindu belief that all people are born into a certain social class on the basis of merit and demerit in their earlier lives.

church
(1) The worldwide community of Christians. (2) A local community of Christians. (3) A worldwide or national Christian grouping, also called a denomination. (4) A building in which Christians meet.

conversion
The change people go through when they leave their former lifestyles in order to live as followers of Christ.

covenant
An alliance in Christian parlance particularly the relationship God initiates with Abraham, Israel and the church, in which God gives them a special status and calling.

creation
Both (1) the action of God in creating the universe, and (2) the universe itself seen as created by God.

demon
An evil spiritual power. Christians believe that demons are angels which were created by God, but have become disobedient to their Creator.

disciple
A follower, or more precisely a 'student', of Jesus, whom they see as

their teacher and example; a term often used of the first generation of Jesus' followers, but more generally of all Christians.

ethics
The systematic study of the moral principles and values that should guide human life.

Eucharist
A Christian celebration of a ritual meal in which bread and wine are shared, and which commemorates the death of Christ on the cross; also called Holy Communion.

evolution, theory of
The theory that the universe and life have gradually evolved; this process can be understood either theistically as directed by God or atheistically as the ultimate explanation of the universe's existence.

evolutionism
The worldview that one needs no other explanation for the existence and order of this world than that it has evolved through a blind evolutionary process.

faith
(1) The attitude of trust in God, and (2) the term used of a system of religious belief, most commonly of the Christian faith.

first-fruits
The first 'instalment' of crops gathered in at harvest time.

globalization
The process by which societies in different parts of the world become increasingly interrelated and dependent on one another.

gospel
A Christian term for the good news of what God has done through Jesus Christ for the salvation of humanity.

grace
God's free, undeserved, loving and merciful action towards humankind.

heaven
(1) In biblical cosmology 'heaven and earth' make up the entire universe. (2) The spiritual realm where God rules.

holiness
The attribute of God that denotes his complete distinction from creation; therefore also used for persons and objects that have a special relationship with God (such as 'Holy Scriptures)'.

Holy Communion
See 'Eucharist'.

Holy Spirit
The Spirit of God himself; the third person of the Trinity.

image of God
The Christian understanding of the human being, who exists in a special relationship with God; also used of Jesus Christ.

karma
The Hindu term for the accumulated merit and debt which people build up through multiple reincarnations and which determines the lives they live.

kingdom of God
A biblical term for the reign of God. Also called the 'kingdom of heaven'.

Lutheran Church
The Protestant denomination originating in the teaching of the sixteenth-century German theologian Martin Luther.

materialism
(1) The worldview based on the belief that the material universe is the only reality that exists. (2) The attitude that sees the acquisition of material goods as the most important goal in life.

Messiah
The Jewish title for the expected liberator and king who was to come to save Israel and humanity; Christians believe that Jesus of Nazareth is this promised Messiah.

miracle
An extraordinary event which Christians experience as an act of God for their benefit; it may, but does not necessarily, suspend the laws of nature.

mission
Christians' outreach to the world to share with others the experience of the salvation they have received.

monotheism
The belief that there is only one God.

multiculturalism
People from different cultural backgrounds living together in the same society and continuing to observe their varied cultural traditions.

mysticism
Religious movements that seek a spiritual encounter with the divine in the depths of the human soul.

myth
A story, often placed in the distant past, which expresses basic religious convictions about the nature of reality and of human existence.

new covenant
The new alliance between God and humanity promised by the prophets in the Old Testament and, Christians believe, inaugurated by Jesus Christ.

New Testament
Literally 'New Covenant'; the second main part of the Christian Bible.

nirvana
The Buddhist term for the ultimate goal of human existence, which involves liberation from the cycle of rebirth, and the end of personal conscious existence and thus of all suffering.

Old Testament
The first and larger part of the Christian Bible, which Christians share with Judaism.

orthodox
Doctrinally correct, the opposite of 'heretical'. When spelled with a capital, it denotes the Christian churches around the east of the Mediterranean Sea that seek to preserve the tradition of the Greek-language theology of the first centuries of the church.

parable
A type of story drawing on situations in everyday life, told by Jesus to explain truths about the kingdom of God.

Paradise
A term used by Christians and Muslims for the blessed state of the first human beings before sin entered into the world, and for the blessed state believers will enter after the last judgment.

Pentecost
A Jewish feast celebrating the first-fruits of the harvest, celebrated by Christians because on the first Pentecost after Jesus' resurrection God gave his followers the gift of the Holy Spirit.

Pentecostal movement
A Christian movement that began in the early twentieth century and that places much stress on receiving the gifts of the Holy Spirit, such as speaking in tongues, prophecy and miraculous healing.

polytheism
The belief that there are many gods.

postmodernity
The culture that has followed modernity – the culture that began with the European Enlightenment or 'Age of Reason' (see above) – and is both critical of and a consequence of modernity.

Protestantism
The religious movement that began as a protest against abuses in the church in the sixteenth century and embraces a wide range of subgroups.

providence
The belief that God takes care of the universe and humankind.

pseudo-religion
A system that is not a religion, in that it does not believe in a reality beyond this physical world, but that functions like a religion in that it claims to present absolute truths and promises ultimate happiness.

redemption
A Christian term for the salvation and liberation God brings from sin and death, which has its origin in the idea of liberating someone from slavery.

Reformed tradition
The Protestant Church tradition originating with the sixteenth-century Swiss reformer John Calvin.

regeneration
The renewal of individual lives by the Holy Spirit when people put their faith in Jesus Christ.

reincarnation
The belief that a person goes through a series of lives.

religious pluralism
(1) The situation in which adherents of different religions live closely together. (2) The position that all major religions are equally valid.

revelation
(1) The act of God in making himself known to humankind. (2) The result of that act of revelation through which God can be known: 'The Bible is God's revelation.'

Roman Catholicism
The church tradition that aligns itself with the authority of the pope in Rome.

sacrifice
A religious practice in which gifts are offered to God or a god, often an animal that is killed, in order to restore a relationship with this God or god; Christians see Jesus Christ's death metaphorically as a sacrifice reconciling humanity with God.

Satan
Christians believe that Satan is the main evil spirit and, like the other demons, a disobedient angel of God.

Scriptures
The Bible, the collection of foundational texts of the Christian faith that describe God's relationship with humankind; other religions have their own 'Holy Scriptures' they consider foundational, such as the Qur'an or the Vedas.

secularization
The process, which has been going on for centuries in Europe, whereby the influence of religion in society is waning.

self-sufficiency
When used of God, this term speaks of his being in need of nothing outside himself.

social contract
The modern Western idea that societies are based on an implicit contract of independent individuals who choose to live together in a society in such a way as to promote the common benefit.

synagogue
A building in which Jews meet to read the Scriptures and pray; Jews began meeting in synagogues before the New Testament times and still do so today.

theologian
Someone who specializes in studying and teaching about God and his relationship with humankind.

totalitarianism
The ideology which gives the state absolute authority over all areas of life and society, forming a totalitarian state.

Trinity (tri-unity)
The Christian belief that the one God and Creator of the universe exists

n some mysterious way as a relationship of three persons, Father, Son and Spirit, who are all equally and entirely God.

utopia
The ideal society some ideologies expect to come in the future.

worldview
The basic convictions that make up a certain outlook on the world and life and that are at the heart of religions and ideologies; for example a Christian worldview or a secular humanist worldview.